Where
Needs
Meet
Rights

Where Needs Meet Rights

Economic, Social and Cultural Rights in a New Perspective

Berma Klein Goldewijk and Bas de Gaay Fortman

Risk
BOOK SERIES

WCC Publications, Geneva

Cover design and photo: Rob Lucas

ISBN 2-8254-1319-4

© 1999, WCC Publications, World Council of Churches,
150 route de Ferney, P.O. Box 2100
1211 Geneva 2, Switzerland
Web site: http://www.wcc-coe.org

No. 88 in the Risk Book Series

Printed in Switzerland

Table of Contents

Introduction

The vulnerability of the growing number of people around the world who are displaced by internal conflict, trapped in poverty and disoriented by global processes of change has underscored anew the importance of economic, social and cultural rights. Yet the meaning and implications of these rights have not been well clarified. New perspectives and strategies are needed to promote a broader recognition of economic, social and cultural rights and to advance, protect and defend them in a concerted way. The urgency of finding such dynamic and integrative approaches has led to the writing of this book.

The argument in brief

Traditional human rights strategies are of limited effectiveness in responding to violations of economic, social and cultural rights. In this book we develop alternative approaches. We start from human needs. Both felt and expressed needs represent what people perceive as want and deprivation. In some contexts, the needs priority may be protection against torture; in other contexts it is food, work, housing, health or education. Our point here is that basic human needs, in particular *unmet needs*, be recognized and expressed in human rights language. So we explore the tension between needs and rights. We discovered that conceptualizing needs in the language of rights highlights the fact that meeting these needs is a social goal which has priority in terms of the common good or the public interest. This makes it possible to identify the rights-holders and to take further action. Indeed, people's participation in matters which affect them is indispensable to the protection of all human rights.

Of decisive importance is that human rights concepts embody *human dignity*. Violations of people's needs must be understood fundamentally as humiliation and dehumanization resulting from deprivation of their fundamental freedoms and basic entitlements. It is important here to go beyond rhetoric and to strengthen the expectation of society that such needs ought to be met: that the dignity of each and every human being must be *respected* and the dignity of the most vulnerable people actively *protected*.

A new momentum

One sign of new momentum in the field of economic, social and cultural rights is the unparalleled importance given by the post-apartheid South-African constitution (1996) to economic, social and cultural rights. Its Bill of Rights enumerates eight social and economic rights: the right to an environment that is not harmful to health and well-being, labour rights, the rights to adequate housing, health care, food, water, social security and education. It also establishes a Human Rights Commission with powers to investigate and report to parliament on the observance of human rights, and to take steps to secure appropriate redress where human rights have been violated. Other signs include the Economic, Social and Cultural Rights Violations Project, launched by the American Association for the Advancement of Science and Human Rights Information and Documentation Systems in 1996; the founding in 1993 of the Center for Economic and Social Rights (CESR) in New York; the activities of the People's Decade for Human Rights Education; and the work of the Maastricht Conference.

International and local non-governmental organizations, including some working outside the human rights field, are becoming more active in addressing economic, social and cultural rights. A gradual shift can be seen in policy of some NGOs with a traditional civil-political focus – such as Human Rights Watch – towards economic and social rights. Others, such as the International Commission of Jurists (ICJ), already have a long record of pressing for the implementation of economic, social and cultural rights. Institutions such as the World Bank and the United Nations Development Programme have also acknowledged the relevance of these rights on the global agenda.

But it is not enough to incorporate human rights language into policy statements. Even experienced human rights organizations continue to face serious dilemmas regarding the implementation and monitoring of economic, social and cultural rights. Recent developments in Asia, Africa and Latin America have shown a weakening of the basis of the state and a corresponding reduction of its ability effectively to support people's living conditions. Where no clear government authority exists, the formulation of integrating perspectives and innovative strategies to implement economic, social and cultural rights is a particular challenge for the international human rights movement.

Thus this book is not just about global policy and strategy, but about building new perspectives and thus creating a broader common understanding of the relationship between needs and rights. Needs and rights meet when they are related to explicit social goals or expectations of society. In the process, needs become a *legitimate* basis for acquirement. This requires concerted strategies and action in society.

What are economic, social and cultural rights?

Economic, social and cultural rights include the rights to an adequate standard of living, to housing and to education, to work and to equal pay for equal work, the rights of minorities to enjoy their own culture, to practise their own religion and to communicate in their own language. But while international treaties recognize the rights to food, health and housing, for example, these are interpreted, explained and understood in terms of the formula of "progressive achievement". In theory, human rights are interrelated, interdependent and indivisible: one right may depend on the realization of other rights for its fulfilment. In practice, however, most approaches and resources have been oriented towards civil and political rights. These rights must be implemented immediately, and state obligations in this respect are absolute. The articles on economic, social and cultural rights in the Universal Declaration of Human Rights (for example, Article 25 on the right to a decent standard of living) are formulated in fundamentally the same way as the other articles ("Everyone has the right to..."). However, the International

Covenant on Economic, Social and Cultural Rights uses the much weaker language of progressive achievement of these rights. While the possibility has been discussed of strengthening the legal character of the obligations under this Covenant,[1] they are generally regarded not as legally binding standards with immediate effect but merely as obligations on a state to take steps "to the maximum of its available resources" (Art. 2).

The first two treaty-based mechanisms to promote the realization of human rights are the two covenants adopted by the United Nations General Assembly in 1966: the International Covenant on Civil and Political Rights (ICCPR) and the International Covenant on Economic, Social and Cultural Rights (ICESCR). These came into existence nearly 20 years after the Universal Declaration was adopted, and did not enter into force until ten years later, in 1976. They contain different supervisory mechanisms, such as inter-state complaints, individual or group petitions and reporting by the states which are parties to them. According to Philip Alston, former chair and now special rapporteur of the UN Committee on Economic, Social and Cultural Rights, *reporting* is the only implementation mechanism specifically provided for in the ICESCR.[2]

National and international legal systems do not have much practice in implementing the economic, social and cultural rights enshrined in international human rights declarations and treaties. To be sure, monitoring committees have been created to clarify and apply the provisions and to communicate with the states that have ratified them. However, monitoring is only one element. Implementation has to do not only with the *reception* of economic, social and cultural rights but also with their *further interpretation and clarification*. Formal international and regional human rights declarations, covenants and conventions – whose contents are virtually undisputed – are a useful but not conclusive or exhaustive framework for implementing rights. Human rights must remain open and open-ended. Implementing these rights is a *process*.

Three new approaches

This book develops a new perspective on economic, social and cultural rights and discusses strategies for their implementation. Adequate health and nutrition, access to clean water, employment, education and cultural identity are not just laudable development objectives. They are basic human rights, protected by the Universal Declaration of Human Rights and the ICESCR. We present three complementary approaches, against the background of analyzing constraints on the everyday realization of human dignity.

First, we develop a *dilemma-oriented approach*. Constraints on implementing human rights in various contexts are much better conceptualized in terms of dilemmas than as problems. The dilemmas facing the human rights movement today come from real life, and we examine some of these arising from particular situations of internal conflict and displacement, poverty and vulnerability. These dilemmas resist easy solutions. They often present open-ended alternatives that are neither wholly right or wholly wrong. A dilemma-oriented approach thus differs substantially from problem statements or scenarios presented in case studies, examples and best practices. We present some of the concerns raised by such dilemmas and examine the values ascribed to the different alternatives.

Of course, not all needs justify rights, and it is not need alone which activates a right. To understand this, we develop in the second place a *needs-led approach*. As a precondition of linking needs to rights, we aim at a renewed grounding of needs in human dignity and the prevention of humiliation. Here we offer a double perspective: needs which are basic to human survival, such as food, water and shelter, are universal, but at the same time they are deeply influenced by people's cultural perceptions and values. A needs-led approach to economic, social and cultural rights is thus fundamentally different from traditional resource-led approaches. Before looking at means, it seeks to identify the *unmet* or *denied needs* of the poor. The core of this book is precisely the use of rights language in connection with needs such as the need for health care and the need for food. This has led to much dispute in human rights circles, despite its international acceptance. The *need for health care*, for example, is more concrete, precise and easy to understand than the *right to health*.[3]

Since strategies to implement economic, social and cultural rights may confront malfunctioning entitlement systems, we develop in the third place an *entitlement systems analysis*. A core notion here is *legitimacy*. Where needs are not being met as a result of entitlement failure, action to acquire the necessary goods and services is to be seen as legitimate. This means that implementation must be made more constructive and practical. A special challenge arises when the protection of people's basic entitlements must take place in adverse environments: disintegrating states, bad governments, malfunctioning economies, cultures of domination and submissiveness.

These three approaches obviously go much further than envisaged by the request presented at the World Conference on Human Rights (Vienna 1993):

> to strengthen the enjoyment of economic, social and cultural rights, *additional approaches* should be examined, such as a system of indicators to measure progress in the realization of the rights set forth in the International Covenant on Economic, Social and Cultural Rights. There must be a *concerted effort* to ensure recognition of economic, social and cultural rights at the national, regional and international levels.[4]

Multiple actors

Among the serious constraints facing international realization of economic, social and cultural rights is a purely "vertical" interpretation of these rights. Their implementation is seen solely as a responsibility of sovereign states; and the entire international human rights system reflects the logic of respecting sovereignty. In addition to this, the *horizontal* functioning of these rights must be promoted. The struggle for human rights involves not only states but also international governmental organizations, multinational corporations, non-governmental organizations and international NGOs. These actors also have duties in regard to people's basic entitlements. Several recent UN world conferences have strongly re-emphasized the relevance of intergovernmental and non-governmental activities in the field of economic, social and cultural rights. Along the same line, the UN Development Programme (UNDP) has explored approaches to poverty and development from a *rights* perspective.[5]

But new perspectives make sense only when related to a commitment to generate the political will to implement concrete policies for protecting and promoting economic, social and cultural rights and standards. In practice economic, social and cultural rights are rarely the subject of concerted political action, media campaigns or critical journalism.[6] Successful efforts to promote economic, social and cultural rights demand contributions from those working outside the human rights field, taking into account living traditions as well as the cultural roots – or uprootedness – and vulnerabilities of affected populations. This implies a human rights culture, a "lived awareness" of human rights principles.[7] Violations of basic human rights affect the overall quality of life.

About this book

Within the field of human rights studies, this book proposes to make poverty, displacement and vulnerability the primary concern. This implies not only addressing such realities in terms of economic, social and cultural rights but also linking human rights discourse to other languages of resistance. Here an important part can be played by priorities regarding economic, social and cultural rights set by NGOs and churches (which are not ordinary NGOs), opinion leaders and political decision-makers. It is precisely a focus on needs and rights that may challenge those involved in international affairs and in alternative development policies and strategies to direct their efforts towards the implementation of economic, social and cultural rights.

For several years the two authors have actively worked together in research and teaching, preparing conferences and symposia, discussing different points of view and elaborating perspectives such as those presented here. While we have opted in writing this book for separate authorship of the different chapters[8] – each working in the areas of our own affinities, skills and experience – the book is not a set of discrete articles. Each chapter was explicitly written to unfold our core argument: that where needs meet rights, humanity is challenged to respect the basic human dignity of all and to protect the dignity of the most vulnerable.

NOTES

[1] See Willem van Genugten, "The Use of Human Rights Instruments in the Struggle against (Extreme) Poverty", paper presented at the CROP/IISL Workshop on Law, Power and Poverty, Oñati, Spain, 11-13 May 1995, p.3.

[2] Philip Alston, "Implementing Economic, Social and Cultural Rights: The Functions of Reporting Obligations", *Bulletin of Human Rights*, 89/1: *Implementation of International Human Rights Instruments*, Geneva, UN Centre for Human Rights, 1991, p.8.

[3] See Brigit C.A. Toebes, *The Right to Health as a Human Right in International Law*, Antwerp, Groningen, Oxford, Intersentia-Hart, 1999.

[4] A/CONF. 157/23, 12 July 1993, para. 98, Part II.

[5] Cf. *Integrating Human Rights with Sustainable Human Development: A UNDP Policy Document*, New York, Communications Development Inc., 1998.

[6] J. Oloka-Onyango, "Beyond the Rhetoric: Reinvigorating the Struggle for Economic and Social Rights in Africa", *California Western International Law Journal*, Vol. 26, No. 1, Fall 1995, p.1.

[7] Joseph Wronka, "Creating a Human Rights Culture: Implications for Peace", *Peace and Conflict Studies*, Vol. 2, No. 1, 1995, p.40.

[8] Chapters 1-2 and 9-10 were drafted by Bas de Gaay Fortman, the Introduction and chapters 3-8 by Berma Klein Goldewijk.

1. Re-examining Economic, Social, Cultural Rights

> The international human rights movement is facing growing problems of irrelevance to people's daily concerns, marginalization in local and global politics, and cooptation by ruling elites, privileged classes and global economic forces in local as well as global politics. In order to resolve these problems, the movement needs to critically re-examine some of its assumptions and policies in order to recapture its original mandate, revise its concepts and methods.[1]
>
> Abdullahi An-Na'im

In 1998 more than one billion people in the world had to survive from day to day without access to clean water and decent shelter. Eight hundred million lacked health services. Almost one billion were illiterate.[2] Yet in 1998 the world also celebrated the 50th anniversary of the Universal Declaration of Human Rights, which says:

> Everyone has the right to a standard of living adequate for the health and well-being of himself and of his family, including food, clothing, housing and medical care and necessary social services, and the right to security in the event of unemployment, sickness, disability, widowhood, old age or other lack of livelihood in circumstances beyond his control... (Art. 25). Everyone has the right to education... (Art. 26).

These strong formulations originate in the words of US President Franklin D. Roosevelt in his State of the Union Address of 1944: "True individual freedom cannot exist without economic security and independence. Necessitous men are not free men."[3] What economic security meant Roosevelt spelled out in a list of rights – to food, clothing, health, education and employment – which he said should have the same status as those incorporated in the US Constitution by the original Bill of Rights of 1791.[4] Indeed, Roosevelt called for a second Bill of Rights as "a basis of security and prosperity for all – regardless of status, race or creed".

A rights-based approach to social and economic security implies that people's access to basic needs is protected by law and legal mechanisms. Of course, this is not the only way of protecting this access. It may also be secured by belonging to communities with social systems based on enduring solidarities, or by less far-reaching alliances with others, or by submission to landlords or others who reward loyalty with benevolent protection against impoverishment, or simply by depending on the well-meaning charity of the haves. But it was clear in 1944 that for masses of people these alternatives offered no prospect of protecting human dignity.

In economies operating on the basis of increasing specialization in production and division of labour, structural protection of interests generally takes the form of law. Hence, to protect people against destitution, basic needs would also have to be protected by law. Just as the "barbarous acts" committed in the second world war, which had "outraged the conscience of mankind" (Universal Declaration of Human Rights, Preamble), so too the material suffering of hundreds of millions of people during the Great Depression of the 1930s encouraged the use of rights language in response to basic human needs.

Yet speaking of livelihood in terms of rights still meets with considerable social, cultural and political resistance. While the Universal Declaration of Human Rights of 1948 is unequivocal ("Everyone has the right to...") about the economic and social rights Roosevelt enumerated, the second Bill of Rights he called for still awaits even a first drafting, and the US, ironically, is among the few countries that have not ratified the International Covenant on Economic, Social and Cultural Rights (ICESCR) of 1966.

The celebration of the 50th anniversary of the Universal Declaration on 10 December 1998 was a rather ambiguous event. While gross and systematic violations of civil and political rights, including frightful occurrences of genocide, still happen, the idea of universal responsibility for the implementation of these rights, involving both states and other actors, has clearly gained ground. States must now account for their observance of these rights; and in cases of violation, local, national and international NGOs come in action to "mobilize shame" (to use a term coined by Amnesty International). But the situation regarding economic, social and cultural rights is far more bleak. In cases of famine and other manifestations of mass suffering of a more material nature, the rights language of the Universal Declaration of Human Rights has generally not been followed by genuine rights-based approaches to evoking concern and meeting people's basic needs. To understand this apparently second-rate treatment of the so-called second generation of human rights, let us first look at human rights in general.

The idea of human rights

The convictions behind the idea of human rights are of course much older than the United Nations. The need to link the execution of power among human beings to norms relating to human dignity is as old as society itself. There is a general consensus that society should *respect* the human dignity of every individual as well as of people living together in communities. To go on to say that *states* should also be called upon to *protect* basic human dignity creates a dilemma, because it is often the very institutions of the state – armies, police forces, "special branches" – which are the most serious violators of human dignity. How can a state which violates human rights be the protector of people's human dignity? Yet the generally accepted opinion is that there is no real choice. It is the state that has the monopoly on executing public justice, if necessary by the use of force. Bodies separate from the public-political realm could not enforce human rights standards.

Notions of fundamental freedoms and basic entitlements directly relating to human dignity are found in diverse cultures. For example, in Chinyanja, a language widely spoken in Southern Africa, there is not a single word for "rights" in the sense of abstract acknowledgments of subjective claims. Fundamental "freedoms" may be translated as *zoyenera za Ufuru wa Cibadwidwe* – all that ought to follow from the freedom of birth – while entitlements grounded in basic needs are *zofunika za Umunthu* – the needs of humanhood. Latin Americans speak of *el derecho por estar en la vida* – "the right to be there".

Although it does not exhaustively enumerate all fundamental freedoms and basic entitlements, the Universal Declaration of Human Rights remains the most authoritative text defining human rights. At the core of these rights are three interconnected aspects: their grounding in *human dignity*, their presentation as *rights* and their inherently *normative* character as principles of legitimacy. This gives them a strength transcending legality (positive law). These characteristics apply to all categories of rights – civil-political as well as socio-economic, individual as well as collective.

The starting point is the acknowledgment of every person's human existence. People count, and in principle no individual counts more or less than any other. There is no special regard or privilege for some; and there are no nobodies, whose human values might simply be neglected.[5] No single human being can be excluded from the *everyone* of the typical human rights texts.

A story from the Hasidic tradition illustrates this. Rabbi Shmuel comes to an inn, where the innkeeper, not aware of the identity of his guest, treats him harshly and disrespectfully. On the Sabbath, in the synagogue, the innkeeper observes the high esteem in which the guest he treated so rudely is held. Approaching Rabbi Shmuel, he apologizes, pleading his ignorance as to the rabbi's identity. The latter replies: "When you harassed me, I thought you knew who I am and that I deserved your behaviour. Now that you inform me of the contrary, I am astonished that you could treat a human being unknown to you in such manner."

Human rights and positive law

The need to respect people's basic human dignity does not merely limit but also governs the execution of power. In modern society this is seen as requiring that the *rights* pertaining to each and every individual human being as well as to communities be stipulated.

The American positivistic tradition in law and political science often distinguishes human rights as "ideals" or "moral rights" from "legal rights". Joseph Wronka, for example, regards human rights implementation as a process from rights as ideals via rights as enactments to rights as exercised.[6] Indeed, if one sees abstract acknowledgments of freedoms and entitlements as rights only in case of effective protection, it is difficult to accept the existence of any pre-existing right at all.

The point of course is that different needs and wants lie behind the rights of different individuals and communities. Rights are the basis of access to resources and commodities. For example, the owner or tenant of a house regularly claims entry to it. Possessing the keys is normally taken as proof of title. In a confrontation with an unauthorized occupant, the police may be called to intervene. If this leads to a legal dispute, the parties will first be asked to prove their respective rights behind the claims. Whose claim will be honoured generally depends on the strength of his or her rights as compared with those of the others. The respective interests and needs behind the rights will be weighed against each other according to such norms such as equity, public justice, equality and legal security.

In a dispute between the owner and the tenant of a house, for example, the judge will not only look at the strengths of the respective rights but also at the interests behind the claims as seen in the light of legal principles. Rights, in other words, do not function as automatic guarantees but rather as *instruments of negotiation and mediation of competing claims*.[7]

Since human rights are directly related to human dignity, they have a strong normativity. On the conviction that they apply to people simply because they are human – and hence do not necessarily require recognition in positive law – human rights may be considered as normally *trumping* other rights. A classic example is the appeal to the higher laws of heaven by Sophocles' Antigone, when she defies King Creon's laws by burying her brother Polynices within the walls of the city. This element of resistance in human rights is also expressed in the Dutch national anthem, in which William of Orange, in his struggle to overcome tyranny, refers to justice as a primary duty towards God, transcending any duty towards an earthly sovereign.

This *supra-legal* element in human rights also implies that those responsible for oppression cannot escape justice by simply appealing to the laws in force during their rule. A recent illustration was the 1996 judgment of the German Constitutional Court regarding officials responsible for assassinating persons seeking to flee the former German Democratic Republic. In regard to these violations of the right to life, the defendants had invoked the principle that there can be no punishment without previous legislation (*nulla poena sine praevia lege*). But the Court concluded that this principle rests on the rule of law, which comprises not just formal but substantial justice, and that those responsible for "extreme injustice committed by the state" (*extremes staatliches Unrecht*) could appeal to the formal law on the basis of which they were acting only as long as that type of state power was actually in force.

It is in societies where human rights have not been incorporated in the existing legal system that these fundamental freedoms and basic human entitlements reach most deeply into people's hearts and minds:

> We Filipinos learned human rights not from books. We were oppressed, and we had no choice but to fight back. In that very struggle we discovered the rights we had lost. We also learned the price that has to be paid to get these rights back. Martial law was a more than adequate teacher in our struggle for civil and political rights. The Philippine movement for human rights was born in this context.[8]

The same is true of economic, social and cultural rights. People discover these rights precisely when those in power neglect claims based on them. Consider, for example, the not uncommon situation in which people are told that they must leave their homes, gardens and the burial places of their ancestors, which about to be flooded by a dam built to supply electricity for national "development". Surely they will base their resistance not only on their interests and needs but on what they see as wrong and right.

The primary requirement of human rights, then, is not *codification* through increasingly refined standard-setting but *implementation* in the sense of day-to-day acceptance of the urgency of people's essential needs as a basis for acquiring the goods and services through which these can be satisfied. Such implementation is an ongoing struggle, regardless of the formal legal status of human rights. Thus, human rights cannot be identified with their role in contemporary international law. Yet, the human rights idea needs a certain incorporation in existing legal systems, just as the international project for the protection of human rights requires constant fertilization from religious and cultural sources.

Economic, social and cultural rights in the UN system

Human rights, as institutionalized with the founding of the United Nations in 1945, were conceived as part and parcel of the attempt by *states* to create a new world order. The massive violation of human rights in the second world war had its background in an ideology – Nazism – that was based on an "us-them" divide.[9] A new world order was needed, with human equality and human dignity as its foundation.

The real impetus for international protection of human rights came with the adoption of the Universal Declaration of Human Rights. As we have seen, it was based to a considerable extent on the thinking of Roosevelt, whose "four freedoms" comprised freedom of speech, freedom of worship, freedom from want and freedom from fear. Such rights, then, take the form of fundamental freedoms and basic entitlements. Regarding core rights – those formulations which evidently relate centrally to human dignity – the Universal Declaration may be considered as part of international customary law of a compulsory nature (*jus cogens*).[10] In the contemporary setting, human rights may thus be seen as *fundamental freedoms and basic needs protected by law*.

Under the United Nations Charter and guided by the Universal Declaration, a so-called *Charter-based mechanism* for the implementation of human rights has been set up, primarily in New York and Geneva, including a Commission on

Human Rights, a Subcommission on the Prevention of Discrimination and the Protection of Minorities and various working groups, independent experts and special rapporteurs. In addition, a *treaty-based mechanism* supervises the implementation of covenants and conventions in specific human rights fields. The 1966 covenants on civil and political rights and on economic, social and cultural rights, together with the Universal Declaration, constitute an "International Bill of Rights".

As noted in our introduction, the International Covenant on Economic, Social and Cultural Rights uses much weaker language than the International Covenant on Civil and Political Rights. Particularly problematic is the terminology of *progressive realization* of the rights specified in the Treaty, which led to the assumption that economic, social and cultural rights were "programmatic, to be realized gradually, and therefore not a matter of rights".[11]

The UN Conference on Human Rights in Vienna in 1993 emphasized that human rights are *interdependent* and *indivisible*. Consider, for example, the connection between freedom of expression and the right to food. What is the meaning of press freedom for people who are suffering from hunger? But the question may also be turned around: what does the "right to food" mean for people who are not free to say that they are hungry? – a situation that occurred in Sudan and Ethiopia in the 1980s, for example. Consequently, all three so-called "generations" of rights – civil-political, socio-economic and collective – should receive equal weight. Yet procedures for implementation and enforcement tend to be most advanced in regard to civil and political rights.

At the beginning of the 1990s, the United Nations discussion of the *progressive realization* of economic, social and cultural rights centred on the issue of *measuring* such "progressive achievements", which led to rather sterile debates on indicators for monitoring country performances. In his final report of 1992, however, Danilo Türk, the Special Rapporteur for Economic, Social and Cultural Rights, went much further, stressing the implications of structural adjustment policies of the international financial institutions for rights protected by the International Covenant. The Commission on Human Rights now spends much more time on socio-economic rights. It has established working groups and appointed independent experts and special rapporteurs for such areas as food, housing, education, extreme poverty, foreign debt, effects of structural adjustment programmes and the right to development. Assisted by the alternative reporting by NGOs, the committee supervising the implementation of economic, social and cultural rights has shown a certain amount of activism in this area, though the terminology of "progressive realization" rather than direct and immediate implementation remains a hindrance.

It may be argued that increasingly refined codification in legal texts, together with the establishment of mechanisms for monitoring compliance, can weaken the moral and rhetorical basis of strategies for implementing human rights. But we would insist that the legally binding character of the Universal Declaration as part of international customary law cannot be undermined by later definitions in human rights treaties.[12] In any event, there has been a recent tendency towards a legal sharpening and strengthening of economic, social and cultural rights, and towards clarifying the justiciable elements of these rights.[13]

The Committee supervising the implementation of the International Covenant on Economic, Social and Cultural Rights argues that the language of progressive achievement "imposes an obligation to move as expeditiously and effectively as possible towards that goal". The Covenant imposes not only "obligations of conduct" ("to promote and to respect") but also "obligations of result" ("to fulfil"). The Committee points out that some of the rights stipulated – for example, the equality between men and women in the enjoyment of economic, social and cultural rights (Art. 3), the right to fair wages and equal pay for equal work (Art. 7), the right to form or join a trade union and to strike (Art. 8), the right to free primary education (Art. 13) – do not depend on a generous endowment of resources but could be realized immediately. States should take the necessary legislative measures and all other "appropriate means" to ensure such rights.[14]

In fact, judicial activism may establish these rights in some national contexts before the legislative and the executive have acted. A striking illustration of the juridically compelling character of these rights comes from the USA, where resistance to talking about socio-economic rights is usually strong. The superior court of California sidestepped the state's own constitution and referred to Article 25 of the Universal Declaration in a ruling that "it defies common sense and all notions of human dignity to exclude clothing, transport and medical care from the minimum subsistence allowance".[15]

Still, in regard to core rights – to food, to health, to work – the text of the Covenant itself points overwhelmingly in the direction of obligations of conduct. Even if interpreted in the strongest possible sense,[16] the formulations do not present the obligations as legally binding standards with immediate effect. No matter how strictly interpreted, a clause such as "to the maximum of its available resources" (Art. 2.1) will continue to imply that the principal focus in concrete cases of violating the right to education or health care, for example, is on raising resource levels rather than on judicial action.

A General Comment written in 1997 by the UN Committee supervising implementation of the Covenant has specified the obligations under the treaty regarding the execution of public policies. The subject was economic sanctions imposed on a country to pressure a governing elite to respect human rights. Noting that such measures severely interfere with the functioning of basic economic, social and cultural rights, the Committee says that this may not result in measures which inflict disproportionate suffering on vulnerable groups within that country:

> Just as the international community insists that any targeted state must respect the civil and political rights of its citizens, so too must that state and the international community do everything possible to protect at least the core content of the eco-

nomic, social and cultural rights of the affected peoples of that state.

In other words, the rationale behind the sanctions may never serve as an excuse to severely affect the living conditions of vulnerable groups. The Committee then regards it as its task

> to scrutinize very carefully the extent to which the state [on which sanctions are imposed] has taken steps "to the maximum of its available resources" to provide the greatest possible protection for the economic, social and cultural rights of each individual living within its jurisdiction... and to take all possible measures, including negotiations with other states and the international community, to reduce to a minimum the negative impact upon the rights of vulnerable groups within the society.[17]

Under no circumstances do the inhabitants of a country forfeit their basic economic, social and cultural rights. This point applies to both the state or states responsible for the initial action and the state confronted with the effects on its resources of the measures taken. That similar obligations apply in the case of economic structural adjustment programmes was, as we have seen, already emphasized by the special rapporteur on economic, social and cultural rights in 1992. While structural adjustment is intended to put the state on a sound financial basis, its effect is often deterioration of the entitlement positions of the weaker sectors of society. Currency devaluation and the resulting inflation reduce the purchasing power of those who are unable to get any compensation in income. The poor are further touched by the removal of food subsidies. Cuts in public spending on health services and education have similar effects. Thus, programmes intended to assist states in achieving a sound basis for a functioning market economy, executed within the context of existing power relations, put disproportionate burdens on the poor, especially women and children. K.O. Rattray concludes:

> Structural adjustment programmes, the natural consequence of which is to cause deterioration in the standard of living of the

vulnerable sectors of the society, constitute a violation of the Covenant for which those [international financial] institutions are liable and accountable.[18]

Yet such authoritative observations have not halted the violation of socio-economic rights through sanctions and structural adjustment programmes. Clearly, mechanisms for implementing human rights will never become self-executing. Human rights is an action-oriented concept, and among human rights, economic, social and cultural rights tend to be even more action-oriented than civil and political rights. The distinction often drawn between civil and political rights as primarily of a *protective* nature, and economic, social and cultural rights as a basis for *positive* action[19] should not be taken in an absolute sense. Nor is it particularly helpful to differentiate between civil and political rights as negative rights, based on *liberty* from interference in the sphere of personal responsibility, and socio-economic rights as positive rights, based on the *opportunity* to achieve a certain quality of life. What, for instance, is the significance of a civil right such as freedom of expression if lack of financial means to publish and disseminate prevents dissenting voices from actually being heard? And what is the meaning of socio-economic rights when structural adjustment programmes imposed by the International Monetary Fund and the World Bank and implemented by national governments result in increasing poverty and starvation?

Beside sanctions and structural adjustment, the increasing violence and displacement within states and the exclusion of people as a result of globalization have re-emphasized the relevance of economic, social and cultural rights on the international human rights agenda. Obviously, a first challenge in implementation is incorporating economic, social and cultural rights into national law, for it is within the national and local context that legal action based on international human rights standards must be undertaken. In itself, however, this is not enough. Such legal resources must be accompanied by socio-cultural and political action to implement human rights in day-to-day life.

The *justiciability* of economic, social and cultural rights is much debated. Since it is difficult to see how such rights can function as objectively perceived entitlements which can be achieved through legal action in courts of law, many jurists refuse to recognize them as real *rights*, suggesting that they function rather as mere *guidelines* (as is implied by the notion of "progressive achievement" in the International Covenant). Yet in cases of people suffering from concrete and specific acts of violation, contentious action may be taken right away. This was done in Zimbabwe, for example, after an entire slum area was demolished to clear the site for a state visit by Queen Elizabeth. As the government had removed the squatters without offering them alternative shelter, the legal aid department of the law faculty of the university summoned the state to court to observe these people's housing rights. Although the litigation failed to realize immediate claims, it contributed to public awareness-building. A more successful effort to implement housing rights took place in the Netherlands in the 1970s. Judicial recognition of squatters' "right to occupy" followed actual occupation of empty premises whose owners were keeping their property merely for speculation. Such social *cum* judicial activism may enhance human rights implementation. When there are clearly identifiable *duty-holders*, socio-economic rights are no less justiciable than civil-political rights.

Organizational constraints

Organizationally, human rights in the UN has become a highly juridical venture, based on standard-setting, monitoring, supervision and adjudication. Human rights is only one of three major enterprises of the UN, alongside collective security and development. Each has acquired its own distinct character. Security became a highly *political* undertaking, with the Security Council as its major institution. Development was conceived primarily in an *economic* setting; it was entrusted to the United Nations Development Programme, as well as to specialized agencies such as the Food and Agriculture Organization, the International Labour Office and the so-called Bretton Woods institutions: the International Monetary Fund and the International Bank for Reconstruction and Development (World Bank). Over the years, these three major international projects have tended to grow more and more apart.[20]

Recently, however, there have been attempts to link aspects of security and development with human rights. In regard to security, one of the first instances was UN Security Council Resolution 688 (1991) on the protection of the Kurdish people in northern Iraq.[21] A more recent example was the authorization of humanitarian action in Kosovo to guarantee observance of human rights, leading the Czech president Vaclav Havel to conclude that the rights of individuals now come above the sovereignty of states.[22] At the same time, the UN Development Programme has sought to qualify conventional economic notions of development with human elements; and its annual *Human Development Reports*, published since 1990, pay attention to aspects of security, good governance and rights. Recently, this has led to the adoption of a "rights-based approach" (the implications of which we shall discuss in the next chapter).

In a legal sense, the universality of human rights is now almost undisputed. All states are bound at least to the UN Charter-based mechanisms, and there is a great deal of international political consensus on the human rights idea, as the Vienna Declaration and Programme of Action of 1993 demonstrated. But serious difficulties remain regarding universal responsibility for the *implementation* of human rights. The Vienna conference itself linked implementation to the need to take account of regional differences and different historical, cultural and religious backgrounds, thus limiting universalist pretensions in regard to realization. While recognizing the universality of human rights as "beyond question", the Vienna Declaration also noted the need to bear in mind "the significance of national and regional particularities and various historical, cultural and religious backgrounds". The Beijing Declaration of 1995 added that implementation is the sovereign responsibility of each state, in "full respect for various religious and ethical values". This beautiful wording conceals an inner contradiction. History has shown that full respect for those values cannot be entrusted solely to individual sovereign states.

Regarding economic, social and cultural rights, the legal method has resulted in strict interpretations of state obligations, as elaborated in the Limburg Principles for the Implementation of Economic, Social and Cultural Rights, the Maastricht Guidelines on Violations of Economic, Social and Cultural Rights and the General Comments of the Committee for the International Covenant on Economic, Social and Cultural Rights. These may play a part in the mechanisms of *reporting* which remain the principal procedures for implementation of the International Covenant.[23] Recent attempts have been made to introduce an individual complaints procedure similar to those available with international conventions on civil and political rights, racial discrimination and torture. Citizens of countries which have signed and ratified these can submit complaints on violation of their rights to the respective UN Committees – provided that they have exhausted all domestic judicial remedies. But this idea seems not to have sufficient support, and, in any event, no matter how laudable the idea, such a juridical exercise would be of limited effectiveness for implementing socio-economic rights.[24]

Conclusion

The international project for the realization of economic, social and cultural rights suffers from three serious constraints. The first is the purely *vertical interpretation* of these rights, in the sense that their implementation is seen as only a state responsibility. In addition to processes for the execution of state responsibilities, there is an urgent need to promote the *horizontal* functioning of these rights, involving individuals, NGOs and international bodies as well as states.

The second constraint is the emphasis on the *juridical method*. The meetings of committees, experts and working groups, with their focus on legal formulations, seem far removed from the daily realities of poor and vulnerable human beings, although the opening statement of the Maastricht meeting of 1997 did show an awareness of the reality of economic, social and cultural rights implementation:

> Since the Limburg Principles were adopted in 1986, the economic and social conditions have declined at alarming rates for over 1.6 billion people... The gap between rich and poor has doubled in the last three decades, with the poorest fifth of the world's population receiving 1.4 percent of the global income and the richest fifth 85 percent. The impact of these disparities on the lives of people – especially the poor – is dramatic and renders the enjoyment of economic, social and cultural rights illusory for a significant portion of humanity.[25]

The third obstacle is the one-sided focus on the state's *resource endowment*. Terms like "progressive achievement" create a false impression that there can be just progress in the realization of such rights. This view lies behind conventional development-oriented approaches towards their implementation. What that means in terms of implementing economic, social and cultural rights we shall discuss in our next chapter.

NOTES

[1] A.A. An-Na'im, "Human Rights and the Culture of Relevance: The Case of Collective Rights", in M. Castermans-Holleman, F. van Hoof and J. Smith, *The Role of the Nation-State in the 21st Century: Human Rights, International Organisations and Foreign Policy*, The Hague, Kluwer, 1998, p.3.

[2] These figures are from the United Nations Development Programme's *Human Development Report 1998*.

[3] In J. Israel, ed., *The State of the Union Messages of the President*, Vol. 3, pp.2875,2881.

[4] Cf. an unpublished paper by Arjun Sengupta, UN special rapporteur on the right to development, presented to the UN Commission on Human Rights in March-April 1999: "Towards Realizing the Right to Development: The Elements of a Programme".

[5] Cf. B. de Gaay Fortman, "No Nobodies", in P. Morales, ed., *Towards Global Human Rights*, Tilburg, International Centre for Human and Public Affairs, 1996, pp.117-21.

[6] Cf. Joseph Wronka, *Human Rights and Social Policy in the 21st Century*, Lanham MD, University Press of America, 1992, pp.28-30.

[7] A.A. An-Na'im, *loc. cit.*, p.8.

[8] Mercy Contreras, "Tien jaar na Marcos", in E. de Boer *et al.*, eds, *Wij leerden mensenrechten niet uit boeken: De Filipijnen en mensenrechten in de periode 1986 tot 1996*, Dordrecht, FIDOC, 1996.

[9] Cf. Bas de Gaay Fortman, "Human Rights – Human Efforts: An Inquiry into the Dialectics of Idea and Project", in Erik Denters and Nico Schrijver, eds, *Reflections on International Law from the Low Countries*, The Hague, Kluwer, 1998, p.34.

[10] See H. Meijers and A. Nolkaemper, "De Universele Verklaring van de Rechten van de Mens bevat thans bindend verdragsrecht", *Nederlands Juristen Blad*, Vol. 76, No. 25, 1997, pp.1113-15. This has been disputed in regard, for example, to Article 24 on the right to leisure and periodic holidays.

[11] A. Eide, "Economic, Social and Cultural Rights as Human Rights", in A. Eide, C. Krausse and A. Rosas, *Economic, Social and Cultural Rights*, Dordrecht, Boston, London, Nijhoff/Kluwer, 1998, pp.5, 21-40.

[12] The legal principle *lex posterior derogat legi priori* does not apply when the earlier law is of a compelling character *(jus cogens)* and the later law requests only voluntary adhesion. In general we would argue that the compelling nature of the UN Charter-based mechanisms for the protection of human rights could not have been undermined by formulations in the treaty-based mechanism. Moreover, while the ICESCR naturally addresses "state parties", the subjective rights language of the UDHR is not swept aside.

[13] See Willem van Genugten, "The Use of Human Rights Instruments in the Struggle against (Extreme) Poverty", *loc. cit.*, p.3.

[14] Cf. K.O. Rattray, "Human Rights from the Perspective of Economic, Social and Cultural Rights", paper presented at the Commonwealth Conference on Human Rights Education and Training, the Commonwealth Association, 11-14 September 1995, p.13.

[15] Cited by Joseph Wronka, *op. cit.*, p.6.

[16] A first effort towards strict interpretation of state obligations in the ICESCR was undertaken by a group of international law experts in 1986 with the adoption of the *Limburg Principles on the Implementation of the International Covenant on Economic, Social and Cultural Rights*. These principles – cf. *Human Rights Quarterly*, Vol. 9, 1987, pp.122-35 – have obviously influenced the General Comments of the UN Committee on Economic, Social and Cultural Rights.

[17] ECOSOC, E/C. 12, 1997/8, 12 December 1997, General Comment No. 8.

[18] Rattray, *op. cit.*, p.19; cf. also John Mihevic, *The Market Tells Them So: The World Bank and Economic Fundamentalism in Africa*, Penang and Accra, Third World Network, 1995.

[19] E. g. by Paul de Waart, *Mensenrechten, Mensenwerk*, Kampen, Kok, 1996, p.11 n.2.

18

[20] Cf. D. van Donkersgoed-Valentine, *A Diamond in the Rough: Towards an Integrated Human Rights Project*, Master's Thesis, The Hague, Institute of Social Studies, Nov. 1994.

[21] Cf. N. Schrijver, "Sovereignty versus Human Rights? A Tale of UN Security Council Resolution 688 (1991) on the Protection of the Kurdish People", in Castermans-Holleman, *op. cit.*, pp.347-57.

[22] V. Havel, "Kosovo and the End of the Nation-State", *New York Review of Books*, 10 June 1999, pp.4-6.

[23] Philip Alston, "Implementing Economic, Social and Cultural Rights: The Functions of Reporting Obligations", *loc. cit.*, p.8.

[24] Cf. Kitty Arambulo, *Strengthening the Supervision of the International Covenant on Economic, Social and Cultural Rights: Theoretical and Procedural Aspects*, Antwerp, Groningen, Oxford, Intersentia-Hart, 1999.

[25] *Maastricht Guidelines on Violations of Economic, Social and Cultural Rights*, Maastricht, 22-26 Jan. 1997, No. 1.

2. Development-Oriented Approaches

> Economic growth does not help the poor much in countries where distribution of wealth is highly unequal. The poor in these countries do not enjoy many of the benefits of boom times, but they do shoulder the costs of collapse. In societies of high inequality, growth allows the poor to keep their heads just above water. When it falls, they sink. [1]
>
> Joseph Stiglitz

Where people lack the possibilities to enjoy the adequate living standard to which Article 25 of the Universal Declaration of Human Rights says "everyone has the right", the solution commonly suggested is *development*. Since this term refers to improvement of a structural nature, it corresponds very well with the idea of "progressive realization" of social and economic rights "to the maximum of available resources". Within the framework of the United Nations and in the policies of governments, the customary focus of such development is understood as the economy.

It is important to distinguish here between economic process, economic structure and economic order. The economic *process* is the actual way in which goods and services are produced, distributed and consumed. The economic *structure* consists of the whole of a country's productive resources in relation to the needs of its population. Productive resources are land and other natural resources, capital goods (factories, roads, harbours, etc.), labour (in terms of both the size of the workforce and its skills) and technical and organizational know-how. The economic *order* is the institutional and organizational framework within which economic activity takes place. Its function is the distribution and way of control of economic power.

A "progressive realization" of economic, social and cultural rights is usually linked to economic growth in the sense of an increase in production over time. The term "development" indicates that this must be rooted in improvement of the economic structure. A rise in the price of oil, for example, will be manifested in economic growth in oil-producing countries, but since it is not based on any improvement in their productive potential, this is not normally seen as development. In its economic interpretation, then, development implies restructuring the economy in such a way that with available resources at least people's basic needs – food, housing, clothing and access to basic health services and education – can be met. Thus, the aim is to lift up resource endowments and to increase *productivity*, that is, output per unit of resource use.

Market-led growth

A *subsistence economy* is one in which all production is directly to satisfy the producers' own needs. People grow their own crops and use the milk of their own cattle. By definition, distribution is direct to those in need, but because of primitive production methods, productivity is inevitably very low. When social and economic rights are not implemented in such a setting, it is due purely to resource constraints. The standard response is to increase productivity by the commercializing of production through specialization and exchange. Local products for subsistence consumption such as maize and rice may also become cash crops; typical export-oriented cash crops include coffee, cotton, tobacco and cocoa.

Productivity in industrialized countries has indeed grown tremendously through division of labour, specialization, technological advancement and economies of scale, significantly increasing average living standards. To be sure, this does not automatically trickle down to eliminate poverty; but the first challenge in this approach remains to increase the cake before trying to share it fairly.

The development strategy based on the idea of "growth before redistribution" is connected to an economic order founded upon free enterprise, open competition and a system of markets and prices. This is reflected in the conviction of the 1991 *World Development Report* of the World Bank that "competitive markets are the best way yet found for efficiently organizing the production and distribution of goods and services".

Strategies of market-led growth have institutional implications. Direct access to resources must be supported by a universalist legal system, in which rules are applied equally in equal cases. Essential is a system of private law, with property and contract as its major pillars. This is not found everywhere. For example, K.L. Karst and K.S. Rosenn have examined the problems arising with the introduction of a universalist legal system in Latin America, with its predominantly "particularistic" legal culture, in which personal connections tend to count for more than a system of rules. This in turn is rooted in the top-down approach by which the rules were introduced and applied in the colonial period, so that "to the elite, law became a norm honoured in the breach. To the unprivileged, law was arbitrary and alien, therefore without moral force."[2]

A market-oriented development strategy implies a general transition from production for people's own needs to what Amartya Sen calls trade-based entitlement.[3] This demands an active role from the state. The establishment of what Adam Smith called an "exact administration of justice" requires a properly trained and independent judiciary to make sure that disputes – which are likely to increase with the transition from a subsistence economy to an economy based on division of labour and exchange – are settled in a way that honours contractual obligations and respects property. The freedom of the market economy is freedom within the law. It is not the freedom to reap another person's harvest or to transfer someone else's produce to your own silo. But in implementing this, society relies as much on general respect for law and order as on courts and bailiffs.

In addition to this legal foundation, trade-based entitlement systems require a physical infrastructure which the state must provide – roads, harbours, airports – as well as public health services and a system of education. Trade-based entitlement systems also require a stable currency, so that both in calculation and in actual exchange entrepreneurs stand on firm ground. So there must be a central bank founded on a high degree of professionalism and guaranteed independence from passing political whims.

What does commercialization imply for people's opportunities for realizing their economic and social rights? While subsistence economies tend, as we said, to have extremely low rates of productivity, socio-economic security in the sense of protection against famine and other disruptions of production is in fact relatively strong. True, self-provisioning is not synonymous with security, but the additional risks of transition to cash crops and trade should not be underestimated. Illustrative is the general transition in Africa from growing cassava (manioc) for subsistence to commercialized maize production. Cassava is a root that can be kept in the ground for a long period and thus used as a reserve crop. Maize depends much more on the rains, and surplus produce in the good years has to be collected from the farm gate. Notably, not all marketing systems work. Commercial maize farmers are also vulnerable to changes in the prices they are paid, which often result from political decisions and not market forces. Consequently, the terms of trade – the relation between the price rural producers receive for a bag of maize and the manufactured products (like clothes) which they can buy for that amount of money – often deteriorates. For example, in the 1960s, peasants in Eastern Zambia had to produce one bag of maize to pay for a piece of cloth (*chitenge*) and two bags for a pair of trousers and a shirt. Now they need two bags.

Hence, in addition to allocation – raising levels of resource endowments – there is the major issue of distribution. As we said, automatic "trickle-down" processes have not been found to work anywhere. This implies yet another role for the state: setting up institutions and mechanisms for the redistribution of income to the benefit of poorer segments of society. Again, this presupposes a legal system with proper law-making and courts of law, as well as a mentality of professional honesty and integrity, particularly among book-keepers, auditors and managers, who play an especially significant role in the market economy.

From the perspective of promoting economic, social and cultural rights, it is important to emphasize these institutional requirements of a functioning market economy. The challenge is not growth of Gross National Product *per se* but improvement of people's basic living conditions. A 1998 United Nations Development Programme report noted that economic growth "continues to benefit many people – indeed, making some unimaginably rich and powerful – but at the same time it has worsened the situation of many others".[4] Economic growth is not an end in itself. It is people who count – and in the first place those who suffer because their basic needs are not satisfied. So what explains the deficiencies of unqualified market-led growth?

The marginalization of traditional institutions

Because subsistence economies suffer from a critical lack of productivity, bringing subsistence farmers into the market economy – a major objective of the World Bank – seems an obvious development strategy. But since by definition subsistence production is directed towards satisfying the producers' own needs, there is no serious problem of distribution. By contrast, a productivity-oriented market economy has serious flaws in distribution. Already in the early days of the development discussion, Dudley Seers showed why a country's Gross National Product can grow rapidly without reducing poverty, unemployment or inequality at all. Indeed, certain types of growth may actually cause social crises and political upheavals.[5] In his study of the rural poor, Ashwani Saith concluded that if the process of growth violates employment and food balances, it "is likely to have regressive distributional consequences".[6]

Development by modernizing the economy often results in violation of economic, social and cultural rights because it negatively affects traditional arrangements of entitlement. Where the legal basis of access to resources changes from traditional institutions – through tribe or clan, for example – to property or other types of private title, the more vulnerable members of the community are likely to be marginalized. This is precisely what happened at the time of the "green revolution" in rural South Asia. As a result of technological developments, people of a less entrepreneurial inclination may easily lose access to land and capital goods. This has been the consequence of agricultural commercialization for the indigenous population in Latin America: they have gone from being subsistence peasants to subsistence workers. Although this implies no change in terms of income poverty, they have become dependent and hence more vulnerable to external forces.

The introduction of trade-oriented entitlement systems, based as they are on civil and commercial law, usually affects the influence of traditional institutions like the tribe, the village and the extended family. Yet traditional institution-based entitlement is not always irrelevant. R. Schott has given a number of examples in which development projects in Ghana failed due to ignorance of traditional entitlement structures.[7] Traditional entitlement tends to be based on communal forms of land-holding rather than on individual titles. This is usually seen as a constraint on commercialization, since it is individual land titles which serve as a security for credits. In terms of the social and economic security of the peasants themselves, however, customary law is not so much to be seen as an obstacle to modernization but rather as a way of protecting economic, social and cultural rights against growing inequality and marginalization. If traditional institutions really have to go, other ways of protecting the weaker members of the community must be found.

Interventionist development policies seek this in state-arranged entitlement systems. Generally, however, where existing systems of enduring solidarities collapse, the state appears unable to replace them with modern institutions attuned to the realization of economic, social and cultural rights. Hence the suggestion that new arrangements be found in *civil society*. However, in many developing countries, especially in Africa, the marginalization of traditional institutions has created a vacuum in this sphere – an absence of strong, well-functioning organizations between the macro-bureaucracies of states and giant corporations and the micro-structures of more or less extended families. To prevent growing inequality and resulting poverty, non-governmental organizations would have to develop strategies to protect people against entitlement failure. But to the extent that such organizations have come into existence, their strategies tend to be based on poverty *alleviation* rather than on implementing economic, social and cultural rights as a foundation for poverty *eradication*. The separation of human rights work from strategies to address poverty still persists.

Despite the generally negative consequences of marginalizing traditional institutions and customary law, there are some cases of what may be called *small capitalism* in which peasants use new market opportunities while their entitlement basically remains within the sphere of customary law. Examples are the introduction of cocoa in Ghana and cotton in Uganda as cash crops for the world market, in both cases preserving some sort of communal title.[8] Whatever measures are taken, the point is that development processes which seek to increase a country's productive potential must provide institutional arrangements to protect people against entitlement failure.

State-led development

In many countries the involvement of the state in development policy has grown out of a desire to accompany political independence by at least some degree of economic independence. Public policies have been initiated using the state as a major instrument of development, directly responsible for allocating resources and producing and distributing goods and services. Too often this has happened even before the state institutions necessary for the adequate functioning of a market economy were in place.

Direct state intervention in the economy typifies an economic order based on central planning. To establish such a system, economic power must be transferred from the private to the collective sector. This implies more rules and authority for individuals in the state bureaucracy. If such officials see their office in terms of personal entitlement and personal duties rather than legal and moral obligations connected to the public interest, the resulting corruption – misuse of office – will mean a deterioration in the entitlement positions of those who depend on the execution of public office. Hence, the easiest way of fighting corruption is to limit office. In a state which is too weak to carry out its policies, enforce its decisions and collect taxes, there may be little alternative. A weak state is no less serious a constraint on development than a totalitarian state which is not subject to the rule of law and in which the government is unconnected to democratic processes of legitimation.

State intervention may manifest itself in taxation, subsidies, incomes policies and price control. If such policies are to protect the purchasing power of the poor, the state must be relatively strong, as well as democratic, in the sense that all citizens, including those in vulnerable socio-economic positions, are involved in the legitimation of public-political power. Whether or not price manipulation benefits the poor depends first and foremost on the orientation and loyalties of those exercising political power. If political power has its roots in the cities, those who benefit from price manipulation are likely to be urban consumers, while rural producers will tend to suffer. Where producer prices are sub-economic, a lot of produce is likely to be sold in black markets, thus expanding the informal economy.

State power may also be used in the sphere of distribution. When development policies result in harmful effects on people's primary entitlement positions, the response is often not to rethink these policies but rather to provide some sort of state-arranged subsidiary entitlement. For example, those who lose their jobs or their traditional access to land receive some sort of compensation. With a relatively strong state such schemes may meet with some degree of success,[9] but weak and undemocratic states are unable to achieve either efficiency or equity in this way.

Particularly in Africa, many states are not only weak but also lack internal legitimacy. R.H. Jackson and Carl Rosberg observe that "the national realm of open, public politics that usually existed for a brief and somewhat artificial period before and immediately after independence has withered and been supplanted by personal power, influence, and intrigue

in most sub-Saharan countries".[10] Processes of democratization after the end of the Cold War have not decisively altered
this. The problem is not so much that state institutions are
ineffective but that they are totally irrelevant except for the
entitlement positions of those attached to them. In societies
where knowing one's rights matters less than knowing one's
friends, state-oriented strategies for development are bound
to fail in terms of both productivity and equity. State power
becomes the dominant social good – in the sense that those
who have it "can command a wide range of other goods".[11]
Under such conditions economic development is seriously
hampered while the political stakes are so high that the struggle for power takes the form of a fierce fight for state-con-
nected entitlement positions. Consequently, it is an illusion
to think of development in the sense of raising national
resource endowments, let alone to look to it for the implementation of economic, social and cultural rights.

In response to the predicament of the state in many
developing countries two different tendencies may be
observed. One is the imposition of structural adjustment programmes. As we saw in the previous chapter, in obliging
governments to take such measures, international financial
institutions must comply with internationally established
norms for human rights. In human rights terminology, this is
a matter of *Drittwirkung* – the way in which the norms
imposed on states affect third parties. In regard to many
rights and freedoms international jurists see *prima facie* evidence of such horizontal effect.[12] Moreover, experience in
Western industrialized countries has shown that policies to
enhance the state's financial and economic solidity will succeed only if forced reductions of the collective sector are
accompanied by a strengthening – not a weakening – of the
state institutions essential for an adequately functioning
market economy.

A second type of reaction to the problem of an overbur-
dened weak state is to replace state-arranged entitlement
with new frameworks for the transfer of resources which are
administered by non-governmental development organiza-

tions. The snag here has been noticed by Saith, in relation to rural poverty:

> Bootstrap operations and self-help schemes abound and are intended to provide an appropriate institutional framework for generating a reoriented pattern of development. However, these schemes even collectively constitute a very minor change... In addition, virtually all such non-governmental development organizations carefully circumvent most structural issues to do with the organization of labour as a collective countervailing force, or to do with access to laws.[13]

Even if his final observation overstates the situation, Saith certainly has a point. Where processes of entitlement require collective action by citizens for the provision of collective goods, non-governmental development organizations tend to be poor substitutes for state institutions. Often they operate in a sphere where power is rooted in relations to foreign donors rather than in direct relations within the society in which they are working. A typical role is in the construction of civil society in an economy where subsistence production is gradually being replaced by division of labour, specialization and exchange. Thus it contributes to institution-building of a different nature from that of directly providing collective goods and services. In the short term, however, such organizations are definitely faced with a dilemma. For example, millions of pupils would be deprived of primary education if the Bangladesh Rural Advancement Committee (BRAC) – a mega-NGO – were to give up its programmes in that sector. At the same time, these programmes allow the government to neglect its own educational task and spend more money on the army. We shall return to the issue of such dilemmas in the next chapter.

Non-governmental development organizations cannot fully solve the problem of entitlement failure where national states are weak. Nor can they replace the state in its function as guardian of personal security – and freedom from want cannot be separated from freedom from fear.[14] The kind of regional integration brought by the European Union might help some national states unable to carry out essential economic and financial policies, but for most developing countries such supra-national institutions have yet to be formed. For those concerned with economic, social and cultural rights, the decline and fall of already weak states remains a cause for great concern.

It is evident that development-oriented approaches to the "progressive realization" of economic, social and cultural rights encounter serious obstacles. Genuinely raising a country's resource endowments implies significant institutional requirements. Moreover, development policies often create their own problems in the area of protecting people's basic human needs. Such deficiencies have led the United Nations Development Programme to acknowledge unequivocally that poverty "is not merely a grave social and economic problem but also constitutes a violation of human rights".[15] This has led to the adoption of a *rights-based approach*, which sees eradicating mass poverty as being as much "a political challenge as an economic challenge, since it requires political stability, conflict prevention, sound governance and political will".[16] This approach to poverty implies policies aimed at political stability, conflict prevention and good governance: an "enabling environments" strategy.

Enabling environments approaches

In contrast to a strategy for implementing human rights by redressing specific acts of violation on a case-by-case basis, an "enabling environments" approach seeks to promote the observance of human dignity by measures which enable people to exercise their rights under the law from day to day. We saw in the preceding chapter that while concrete and specific violations of socio-economic rights are no less *justiciable* than violations of civil and political rights, the language of the International Covenant on Economic, Social and Cultural Rights points rather to structural issues. Consequently, situations of structural non-implementation of socio-economic rights tend to receive more attention than specific acts of violation. What is new is a realization that such conditions do not just follow from resource limitations but are also related to major deficiencies in the institutional environment – the economy, the polity, society and culture – in which human rights are to be implemented.

The term "creation of *enabling environments*", coined by the United Nations Social Summit in Copenhagen in 1995, suggests that rather than waiting for concrete violations to be addressed, those seeking to promote human rights should enhance the conditions within which people are able to exercise their rights under the law. The United Nations Development Programme has identified three "entry points" for its enabling environments approach to human rights implementation: a focus on disadvantaged groups in society, support to peace-building, and promotion of democratization and the institutions of good governance, including human rights institutions.[17]

For the UNDP, an enabling environment is intrinsically linked to *human* development. The adjective "human" underscores that functioning markets have never been enough to cope with intolerable living conditions. Human development implies that individuals and communities can follow their own orientations while increasing their options. Economic growth remains a basic indicator of human development, but supplementary indicators are also used, especially health (average life expectancy, infant mortality) and education (literacy rate). Human development thus acknowledges that life is more than a mere continuous struggle for survival. Here it is useful to recall the words of Adam Smith, the ideological founder of the free market economy:

> Commerce and manufactures gradually introduced order and good government, and with them, the liberty and security of individuals, among the inhabitants of the country, who had before lived almost in a continual state of war with their neighbours, and of servile dependency upon their superiors.[18]

Clearly, Adam Smith saw economic development as a precondition of *security*. Security has to do with the many threats people face in their lives. In a broad sense, it entails safety. Safety implies *protection* against disaster; security adds the dimension of *prevention*: a minimization of threats to human existence and co-existence. Thus, security means freedom from disaster, anxiety, attack and violent disruption of what is considered a "normal" life.

Yet there may be as many perceptions of a normal life as there are people on our planet; and security is thus a contested concept. Contradictions arise over the relations between defence and security, between individual, national and international security, and between violent means and peaceful ends. Every period in human history seems preoccupied with its own specific interpretations of security. During the Cold War, for example, the emphasis was almost exclusively on security between states.

The UNDP's 1994 *Human Development Report* points to a new notion of security: security between people rather than just between states. The components of this notion of *human security* are economic, food, health, environmental, personal, community and political security. Specifically, the report attempts to unite the two pillars of security: freedom from want and freedom from fear.

The quest is thus for a new paradigm of sustainable human development that encompasses security and human rights. While human security implies peace and stability, development is seen as a process of extending people's range of choices. The relationship between human development and human rights is obvious. In the first place, human rights comprise socio-economic rights. Furthermore, human development is part of the institutional context within which human rights, including civil-political rights, are to be implemented. Indeed, it is striking that it is precisely in the countries at the bottom of the ranking in the UNDP's Human Development Index where human rights violation tends to be gross, severe and systematic.

Furthermore, in countries where the polity is not functioning, human rights observance generally tends to be very low. "Ungovernment" or bad government implies that law plays a marginal or even oppressive role, while the exercise of state power is not subject to the rule of law. Earlier we cited Adam Smith's emphasis on the "exact administration of justice" as a major responsibility of the state. Today, even the World Bank admits that more is needed than merely market freedom. As its 1997 *World Development Report* says, "An effective state is vital for the provision of the goods and services – and the rules and institutions – that allow markets to flourish and people to lead healthier lives." In a positive sense this is called *good governance*. If we see democracy as processes for representative, participatory and accountable government – Abraham Lincoln's "government of the people, by the people and for the people" – good governance is primarily related to accountability, in the sense of an adequate distribution of power and its control through systems of checks and balances. In summary, a well-functioning polity means that the state is able to provide collective goods and services and to collect taxes, that it is subject to the rule of law (which implies an independent and accessible judiciary), that those who hold office are accountable (preventing corruption, for one thing) and that political power is not a monopoly of any one group.

Finally, we may note that a functioning state requires a strong civil society in the sense of groups and institutions related to but not part of the state. Also important are relations among the different groups in society, with their often conflicting collective interests. Naturally, an enabling environment implies nonviolent means of settling disputes. Here we touch on a cultural factor in the environment. If at the micro-level of families and small communities cultures of domination and submissiveness prevail, these are likely to be reflected in relations between groups at broader levels. Hence, an enabling environment for the observance of human rights would have to include cultures of participation and nonviolence.

Conclusion

"Enabling environments" approaches remain a rather instrumentalist way of tackling the implementation of economic, social and cultural rights. Conventional development-oriented strategies, focused on efforts by states to improve their resource endowments, are supplemented by well-meant attempts to enhance the quality of government. In reality, however, poverty and starvation, high rates of infant mortality, child labour and urban squalor are not caused only by resource limitations and the absence of well-functioning state institutions. It is processes through which individuals or groups are wholly or partially excluded from full participation in the society in which they live that tend to result in lack of livelihood and destitution. This poses the need for *social development*, based on collective action by citizens themselves, to enable societies to improve the quality of life. Indeed, even those who stress the need for macro-economic growth in well-functioning market economies admit that growth can never be more than half the story. Only where the two pillars of development – productivity and entitlement – are intertwined at the level of the people themselves can one speak of human development in the sense of an environment enabling *freedom from want*.

The focus on institutions in development-oriented and related "enabling environments" approaches can mean that people themselves drop out of sight. In implementing economic, social and cultural rights, we are concerned not primarily with countries and economies but with human beings. It is indigenous peoples, foreign migrants, refugees and internally displaced persons, minority and other vulnerable groups that tend to suffer most under policies and actions involving violation of basic entitlements.

The implementation of economic, social and cultural rights is not a matter of simple social engineering and "problem-solving". Such strategies take one problem – resource pressure – as a basis for policy development. The means used to solve that problem easily create new problems, which in turn demand new policies, which create still new problems, and so on. Through such "policy spirals" entire bureaucracies may come into being while the actual suffering of the people whose economic, social and cultural rights are not being realized is not tackled. A problem-solving orientation neglects the dilemmas that tend to manifest themselves at the interface of economy, polity, society and culture. In the next chapter we shall try to develop a "dilemma method" which may contribute towards strategies for the realization of people's basic entitlements.

NOTES

1 J. Stiglitz, "The World's War on Poverty Has Yet to be Won", *International Herald Tribune*, 28 April 1999. See also L. Hanmer, N. de Jong, R. Kurian and J. Mooij, *Poverty and Human Development: What Does the Future Hold?*, ISS Working Paper Series No. 259, The Hague, Institute of Social Studies, Oct. 1997, who conclude from several different scenarios regarding growth and distribution that policy orientation can be as important as economic growth in achieving improvements in human development indicators; p.31.

2 K.L. Karst and K.S. Rosenn, *Law and Development in Latin America*, p.701.

3 Amartya Sen, *Poverty and Famines: An Essay on Entitlement and Deprivation*, Oxford, Clarendon Press, 1981.

4 *Overcoming Human Poverty*, New York, UNDP, 1998, p.15.

5 Dudley Seers, "What Are We Trying to Measure?", in Nancy Baster, ed., *Measuring Development: The Role and Adequacy of Development Indicators*, London, Frank Cass, 1972, p.22.

6 Ashwani Saith, *Development Strategies and the Rural Poor*, Working Paper Series No. 66, The Hague, ISS, Nov. 1989, p.43.

7 See R. Schott, "Law and Development in Africa", in *Law and State: A Biannual Collection of Recent German Contributions to These Fields*, Vol. 24, 1981, pp.30-41.

8 See Bas de Gaay Fortman, "The Dialectics of Western Law in a Non-Western World", in J. Berting et al., eds, *Human Rights in a Pluralist World – Individuals and Collectivities*, Westport, Meckler, 1990, p.240.

9 A. Kohli gives an example of a "Food for Work Programme" in West Bengal; *The State and Poverty in India*, Cambridge, Cambridge UP, 1989.

10 R.H. Jackson and Carl G. Rosberg, "The Marginality of African States", in G.M. Carter and P. O'Meara, eds, *African Independence: The First Twenty-Five Years*, Bloomington, Indiana UP, 1985, p.52.

11 M. Walzer, *Spheres of Justice: A Defence of Pluralism and Equality*, Oxford, Blackwell, 1983, p.10.

12 See Fried van Hoof, "International Human Rights Obligations for Companies and Domestic Courts: An Unlikely Combination", in Castermans-Holleman et al., eds, *The Role of the Nation-State in the 21st Century*, pp.54ff.

[13] Ashwani Saith, *op. cit.*, p.53.

[14] See Emma Rothschild, "What is Security?", *Daedalus*, Vol. 124, No. 3, 1995, p.80.

[15] *Overcoming Human Poverty*, p.15.

[16] James Gustave Speth, "Poverty: A Denial of Human Rights", *Journal of International Affairs*, Vol. 52, No. 1, Fall 1998, p.283.

[17] *Ibid.*, pp.288-91; cf. also the UNDP policy document "Integrating Human Rights with Sustainable Human Development", Jan. 1998.

[18] Adam Smith, *An Inquiry into the Nature and Causes of the Wealth of Nations*, London, 1776.

3. A Dilemma Approach to Human Rights

> Dilemma... implies humility in the presence of life's complexity, an acceptance of the limitations of human knowledge, an anguish at the possibility of losing one value when choosing another value.[1]
>
> Godfrey Gunatilleke

Dilemmas manifest the contradictory nature of reality. They reveal conflicting objectives and difficult orientations between alternatives. And they resist easy solutions. In this chapter we shall identify some dilemmas in the field of economic, social and cultural rights and their implementation.

However, a systematic approach that provides guidance in handling dilemmas in the field of human rights has not yet been explored. In developing a conceptual framework for a *dilemma approach* to human rights, our basic hypothesis is that such an approach will be much more effective than problem-oriented approaches in giving priority to the vulnerability of various groups of people in everyday life. Choices and commitments should thus be situated in the context of dilemmas, not seen in terms of problems demanding resolution. Indeed, there are no simple responses to the paradoxical character of human existence as such.

Resource and vulnerability dilemmas

The dilemmas facing the human rights movement today arise out of highly complex and open-ended real-life situations with no clear guidelines, no map or compass to guide us through them. On the contrary, dilemmas that emerge from concrete reality are often confusing and stressful precisely because they are linked to different and conflicting ways of settling matters. Complex dilemmas also reveal a wide "grey area" regarding the appeal to ethical principles. It may be easy to identify right and wrong by relying on general ethical principles and values such as respect, justice, fairness and responsibility, but dilemmas in real life often present open-ended alternatives that are neither wholly right nor wholly wrong.

The resource dilemma

One of the most concrete and painful dilemmas in understanding the meaning and implementation of economic, social and cultural rights is the resource dilemma. On the one hand, there is the right to food, internationally enshrined and endorsed through ratification by most countries. On the other hand, there is the inability of poor states to provide everyone an adequate level of food or the necessary economic and political development. The same can be said about the right to health or housing or work or education. Impediments to improving the food system within a state may range from misallocation of resources to inefficiency and negligence to corruption and carelessness. Nevertheless, each state which is a party to the International Covenant on Economic, Social and Cultural Rights undertakes to "take steps, individually and through international assistance and cooperation, especially economic and technical, to the maximum of its available resources, with a view to achieving progressively the full realization of the rights recognized in the present Covenant by all appropriate means" (Art. 2.1).

Of course, the "available resources" for some states are very limited in comparison to those for others; and this formula can easily be misconstrued as suggesting that they thus have few if any obligations and responsibilities under the Covenant. However, *all* ratifying states are obliged to respect economic, social and cultural rights, notwithstanding their level of economic development. The dilemma as such appears to be foreseen in the reference in the Covenant to the probability that states will have to call upon international assistance. Of course, resources will vary. But as the Limburg Principles on the Implementation of the International Covenant on Economic, Social and Cultural Rights, adopted in 1987 by a group of experts in international law, state: "The obligation of progressive achievement exists independently of the increase in resources; it requires effective use of resources available."

This was affirmed even more strongly by the UN Committee on Economic, Social and Cultural Rights itself in its earlier cited General Comment of 1997 on economic sanctions and respect for economic, social and cultural rights. During the 1990s United Nations sanctions of varying kind and duration have been imposed on South Africa, Iraq, parts of the former Yugoslavia, Somalia, Liberia, Haiti, Angola, Rwanda and Sudan. The Committee on Economic, Social and Cultural Rights has no part in the decision to impose sanctions, which is the entire responsibility of the Security Council. The Committee, which is responsible for monitoring compliance by all parties to the Covenant, stated that

> the provisions of the Covenant, virtually all of which are also reflected in a range of other human rights treaties as well as the Universal Declaration of Human Rights, cannot be considered to be inoperative, or in any way inapplicable, solely because a decision has been taken that considerations of international peace and security warrant the imposition of sanctions (General Comment No. 8, 1997, para. 7).

On the face of it, there appears to be no escape for states:

> To the extent that sanctions are imposed on states which are not parties to the Covenant, the same principles would in any event apply given the status of the economic, social and cultural rights of vulnerable groups as part of general international law, as evidenced, for example, by the near-universal ratification of the Convention on the Rights of the Child and the status of the Universal Declaration of Human Rights (para. 8).

Thus in this formulation of the outcome of the resource dilemma, the UN Committee apparently flees from the dilemma itself.

The vulnerability dilemma

Economic sanctions imposed by the Security Council almost always result in grave and dramatic violations of economic, social and cultural rights. They disrupt the distribution of food and sanitation supplies, endanger the quality of food and the availability of clean drinking water, interfere with the functioning of basic health and education systems and undermine the right to work. Sanctions also have politi-

cal consequences: they can reinforce the power of the privileged and the governing elites over the population at large,
while restricting opportunities for asylum.

The dilemma here might be called a vulnerability
dilemma. On the one hand, there is the basic objective of
applying political and economic pressure to persuade the
governing elite of a country to conform to international law.
On the other hand, there is the accompanying suffering
inflicted upon the most vulnerable groups in that country.
This dilemma also is not resolved by the UN Committee;
rather, it appears in the end to be associated with an appeal:

> While sanctions will inevitably diminish the capacity of the
> affected state to fund or support some of the necessary mea-
> sures, the state remains under an obligation to ensure the
> absence of discrimination in relation to the enjoyment of these
> rights, and to take all possible measures, including negotiations
> with other states and the international community, to reduce to
> a minimum the negative impact upon the rights of vulnerable
> groups within the society (General Comment No. 8, 1997, para.
> 10).

By appearing to resolve the dilemma in a double appeal –
for more effective monitoring under the terms of the
Covenant, and for states to assume their responsibility to do
all within their power to protect the economic, social and cultural rights of the affected population – the Committee leaves
the dilemma open.

Equally justifiable alternatives

A dilemma, as the resource and vulnerability dilemmas
make clear, is more than just a choice between two opposing
sides. What characterizes a dilemma is: (1) the existence of
real alternatives that are equally justifiable; (2) the presence
of different values which underlie conflicting interests; and
(3) significant consequences on actors in a specific context.
In other words, we speak of a dilemma when we are faced
with the need to figure out an orientation in the midst of different alternatives. In this sense, there is no easy way out; if
there were, the situation would not be a dilemma.

Implicit in the term dilemma are three concepts: the *alternatives* or poles which are mutually exclusive, the *choice* or option which finally has to be made, and the *implications*. A dilemma approach assumes a situation in which there are *two* poles or alternatives, and the better one cannot be easily identified. Each alternative is valid and important, neither can be sacrificed, and both cannot be opted for simultaneously.

In real-life situations, of course, the options are rarely limited to two.[2] Understandably, then, the objection to a dilemma approach arises that the complexity of a problem should not be identified with and bound to only two possible responses. Framing real-life situations as dilemmas may reduce complexity rather than clarifying it.[3]

The point however is that in many real-life situations a "both... and..." outcome is not possible. Even when a compromise has been found, the character of the dilemma continues to exist: choosing the one alternative makes it impossible to enjoy the benefits of the other possibility. The painful element of a dilemma is precisely that the two real possibilities keep each other in a balance. Taking advantage of the one option, we miss the contribution of the other. In this sense, the form of a dilemma is indeed unavoidably *constrictive*: it reduces the basic options at stake to two.

In sum, a dilemma confronts us with the *inevitability* of weighing against each other two poles, each with its advantages and disadvantages. Whatever the choice, there will be a serious loss because it is impossible to take the other alternative as well. While each of the two conflicting possibilities has a meaning in its own right, neither is fully right nor fully wrong. Thus the underlying value conflict regarding the highest good has consequences for the way out of the dilemma, in which case the possible adverse consequences must also be seen from the pole which is excluded.

The importance of posing a dilemma is that the nature of the choice itself and the reflection about making it are put in the centre of attention. This restores the element of human choice and relates it to the human condition itself. In the field of human rights, this means that making a choice as such cannot be disconnected from the total human benefit and cost. In other words, neither of the two alternatives can easily be sacrificed. At the time the choice must be made, however, the nature of the choice and its outcomes are never perceived in their entirety. Because there can be only one way out of the dilemma, there are always serious implications; the loss of meaning and values present in the other pole always causes human suffering.

Value-conflicts

We have seen that dilemmas are rooted in value-conflicts which manifest themselves in a variety of ways. Thus there are different ways to handle dilemmas related to the implementation of economic, social and cultural rights.[4]

In this connection, we should give some attention to the role of a new actor on the human rights scene: multinational enterprises and the codes of conduct they are developing. The decisions taken by multinationals in the face of specific resource and vulnerability dilemmas affect many aspects of people's lives and influence matters of national and worldwide importance, among them environmental issues. Many companies have begun thinking about their human rights responsibilities, and a few have started to implement policies in this area.[5] The growing sense of corporate responsibility for human rights can be seen as a result of two tendencies: greater recognition of the relevance of international human rights law, and the need felt by multinational enterprises to redefine their role in society in the context of interdependence and globalization.[6]

But the codes of conduct prepared by multinationals have so far had limited effect as a vehicle for a human rights policy. First, they do not always effectively address fundamental problems, such as the use of forced and bonded labour. Second, their protective force seems weak. Ethical standards which the company intends to uphold are set forth, but no basis for legal claims by third parties is offered. Moreover, they do not include complaint procedures or foresee any sanctions or remedies in case of non-compliance. Third, the provisions related to human rights are framed in terms too vague to offer clear guidance in specific situations. Hence, the mechanisms for implementation and monitoring of the codes do not usually provide a high level of transparency and accountability.

Having mentioned these limitations, however, we should go on to say that codes of conduct do offer a significant basis for continuing discussion. It must be recognized in this connection that international law has thus far consisted mainly of rights and obligations for its traditional subjects – sovereign states. International law tends to adapt slowly – but, one may hope, surely – to the realities of the world. In this respect, it must take increasing account of the critical role played by multinational enterprises in all areas of life, all over the world.

Because of inherent value conflicts, dilemmas are persistent and fundamental. Moreover, value conflicts as such are not static but dynamic. Indeed, a dilemma approach to economic, social and cultural rights differs substantially not only from problem statements, but also from scenarios presented in case studies, examples and "best practices". Case studies, for instance, often have a limited explanatory value and may fall short of telling the whole story. Many are simplistic and operate with a static time-frame. Even more serious is the certitude and complacency evident in most accounts of "best practices", which ignore fundamental paradoxes in the human condition and the vulnerability and fragility which so often typify real-life situations.

Dilemmas versus problems

In elaborating a dilemma approach, we are distancing ourselves from ways of thinking, procedures and methods which consider the moment of choice as the ultimate solution of a problem. In a sense, such problem-oriented approaches may be described as "totalitarian", because they disregard the complexity and variety of concrete reality.

> The thought frame in which the choice is always clear and the methodology for finding the right solution for every choice is always available is essentially totalitarian in its outlook... It pro-

vides no outlets for communication with approaches and choices other than its own. In its inflexible search for the good it thus becomes inhumanly oppressive, transforming itself into the opposite of what it desires to be and becoming a source of evil.[7]

Of course, not every problem can be formulated and interpreted in terms of a dilemma. Why should certain choices which have to be made be approached as being embedded in a dilemma? First, the fact of posing a dilemma already means resistance against the tendency in problem-oriented approaches to look for "solutions". Second, a dilemma cannot be reduced to a *decision-problem*, as it appears in many types of management theory, but must be seen as relevant in terms of a *basic orientation* in the midst of conflicting values.

From a managerial perspective, *avoidance* is often seen as the right way to handle dilemmas. This is why corporate circles consider practical tools like codes of conduct, policies, procedures and special training sessions so important.[8] However, approaches which focus on preventing dilemmas or which offer checklists in this regard[9] manifest an interpretation of dilemmas as phenomena that should be circumvented. This negates the persistent and fundamental character of dilemmas.

One might object that a problem can also be interpreted in different ways. However, a problem-based way of dealing with difficult orientations and options eliminates the one pole in function of a solution. The problems at stake will always reappear, repeat themselves in other forms and may even accumulate, simply because heterogeneity has been reduced to, included in or mixed up with the homogeneity of the "solution". Diversity and heterogeneity disappear; all contradictions seem to be resolved. The opposites are not recognized as always being immanent in reality.

Conclusion

We have tried in this chapter to take account of the fundamentally paradoxical character of reality and to provide some basic orientation for handling dilemmas.

These insights into the nature of dilemmas may serve as a basis for a new approach to strategies for implementing economic, social and cultural rights. In this approach, dilemmas are seen as a constitutive and dynamic part of real-life situations. Accordingly, human rights organizations and non-governmental development bodies are challenged to produce tools and instruments for dealing with dilemmas as they arise. From this perspective, the next chapter will deal with a needs-led orientation to human rights.

NOTES

1 Godfrey Gunatilleke, "The Ethics of Order and Change: An Analytical Framework", in Godfrey Gunatilleke, Neelan Tiruchelvam and Radhika Coomaraswamy, eds, *Ethical Dilemmas of Development in Asia*, Lexington MA, D.C. Heath, 1983, p.26.

2 See Caroline Whitbeck, "The Trouble with Dilemmas", *Journal of Professional Ethics*, Vol. 1, Nos 1-2, 1992, pp.119-42.

3 Carol Gilligan, *In a Different Voice: Psychological Theory and Women's Development*, Cambridge MA, Harvard UP, 1982.

4 See Berma Klein Goldewijk, "The Quest for Human Dignity: Religion and Human Rights in a Context of Globalization and Conflict", *Research Seminars States and Societies*, No. 98-17, The Hague, Institute of Social Studies, 1998, p.3; and Kwasi Wiredu, *Cultural Universals and Particulars: An African Perspective*, Bloomington, Indiana UP, 1996.

5 For the recognition by Shell of the responsibility of multinational corporations in the field of human rights, see its "Statement of General Business Principles", in *Profits and Principles: Does There Have To Be A Choice?*, London, AIA/Carterhouse Printing, 1998; and *People, Planet and Profits: An Act of Commitment*, London, Shell International Group on External Affairs, 1999.

6 Cf. *Multinational Enterprises and Human Rights*, a report by the Dutch sections of Amnesty International and Pax Christi International, Utrecht, Nov. 1998.

7 Godfrey Gunatilleke, *loc. cit.*, p.25.

8 In *Profits and Principles* and *People, Planet and Profits*, Shell presents the "Issues and Dilemmas" they are facing, while advocating an approach of dilemma-sharing.

9 Cf. Laura Nash, "Ethics without the Sermon", *Harvard Business Review*, Vol. 59, 1981.

4. A Needs-Led Approach to Human Rights

> We are led to presume that poor people have a greater need for food, clean water and shelter than their need to feel loved by others and respect for themselves. By extension, we also seem to operate on the assumption that there is a hierarchy of psychological functions: that one cannot feel shy, hopeful or humiliated when one is hungry, thirsty or cold. In truth, all these needs operate simultaneously in human beings, and life is lived by people who synchronously exercise their psychological, social and physical capacities.[1]
>
> Linda Richter

Human and basic needs require an ongoing conceptualization of human rights. The realities of violent conflict, displacement, poverty and vulnerability urge a further elaboration of the fundamental standards of humanity and call for new strategies to implement economic, social and cultural rights. In some environments the priority need may be for access to clean water or to health care; in other contexts it may be for work, education or housing. Often, there is a combination of such needs.

In order to clarify the concept of human needs we shall look in this chapter at the dilemma arising from the existence of objective and universal human needs on the one hand, and human need as a subjective and culturally relative concept on the other hand. Should needs be seen as culture-specific preferences? Are all needs social constructs? Our specific concern is with needs that are *denied*, creating poverty and vulnerability. Basic human needs can in fact be so critical that the existence of the need is in itself a violation of elementary human dignity. Basic rights can be said to be those rights which are necessary for the enjoyment of all other rights.[2] In this connection we focus also on the challenges and limitations of the use of human rights language. Does rights discourse provide the best vocabulary for situations in which people's dignity is injured because their basic human needs are not realized?

Felt needs and expressed needs

It is particularly in times of crisis that people recognize the basic human needs in which their human rights are grounded.[3] The need for work becomes especially evident in times of unemployment; the need for free association manifests itself in a pronounced way under oppressive military dictatorships. To clarify what needs are, we distinguish between *expressed needs*, such as sufficient food, adequate shelter, clean water and health care, and *felt needs*, which may not always be expressed because of power relationships and the abuse of people. In real life, of course, expressed and felt needs are very closely interrelated.

To explore this distinction we should first recall the work of Abraham Maslow, one of the earliest and best-known writers on this subject. In his early work Maslow distinguished two categories of need: *basic survival needs* and *growth needs*. Later he developed a theory of the hierarchy of human needs, starting with *biological and physiological needs*, such as air, water, food, shelter, sleep; followed by *safety and security needs*, such as protection from disease and fear; then *needs for love and belongingness*, affiliation with and acceptance by others; *the need for esteem*, both from others and oneself, for feeling competent, gaining approval and recognition; *cognitive needs*, such as knowledge, meaning, understanding and exploring; *aesthetic needs*, such as beauty, balance, form, symmetry and order; *the need for self-realization*, "becoming everything you can be", finding fulfilment and realizing one's potential.[4] Further elaborating this hierarchy, Maslow also made a broader distinction of needs; from the need for safety to the need for social interaction to the need for transcendence.

Efforts to rank human needs in this way have provoked considerable discussion. Some have proposed hierarchies which identify three levels of human needs: material (physiological, safety), social (belongingness, esteem) and spiritual; others have defined the three levels as physiological, belongingness and self-actualization. Still others have proposed a classification which is not necessarily prioritized: the need for autonomy, the need for competence and the need for relatedness.

One of the difficulties with the hierarchy of needs posited by Maslow and later writers is the tendency to suggest that needs for belongingness, self-esteem and transcendence become relevant only when the needs for food, water, shelter and safety are already met. In fact, all these needs manifest themselves simultaneously.[5] Gradually, more emphasis has come to be given to the interrelatedness of human needs; and the focus has shifted to how needs are connected to social policy.[6]

To explore this perspective further, let us turn back to the distinction between *expressed needs* and *felt needs*.[7] Regarding the gap between felt and expressed needs, it seems appropriate first of all to try to discover what people want, to identify needs and to discover how these needs could be met. However, what is felt cannot always be expressed openly because of oppressive regimes, fear of political repression or disempowerment. Felt needs can also be hidden when they are reformulated to correspond to the available resources or criteria of the development agencies which support them. In this way, needs are sometimes distorted and abused to justify disastrous social policies (an example is unpopular public housing projects).[8] Here one may speak of *prescribed needs* – determined and imposed by professionals or planners rather than by those who feel the need.

In the context of human rights, the notion of *expressed needs* is rather straightforward; and examples of these are found throughout the Universal Declaration of Human Rights: needs for food, clothing, housing, medical care (Art. 25), productive-creative needs (Art. 23, on the right to work), a need for personal security (Art. 12, on the right to privacy), the need for self-actualization (Art. 26, which links education to full development of the human personality), spiritual needs, such as freedom of thought, conscience and religion (Art. 18).

But when organizations try to identify needs, they often define them in terms of available resources already provided. Methodologies for assessing needs tend to use information-gathering techniques developed in the field of management. Such methodologies are often part of broader needs analyses used in programme-planning and decision-making processes.[9] The crucial issues in this context are who determines the availability of resources, which indicators of need are employed and who will use the information about needs. Such needs assessments often use data in the form of social indicators taken from statistical information and surveys of the target population. In short, needs are identified in *instrumental terms* using bureaucratically or professionally defined categories.

The point we wish to make is that when people's basic needs are unmet, they are affected in their *basic human dignity*. Instead of ranking needs by constructing hierarchies and priorities – as managerial approaches tend to do – we aim at a renewed grounding of needs in human dignity and humiliation, as a precondition of linking needs to rights. This however is not without its difficulties. Needs are deeply influenced by people's cultural perceptions and values. Needs which are basic to human survival – food, water, shelter – are universal, but they are elaborated in culturally conditioned ways.[10] Hence, needs approaches must start from this double perspective. Several steps seem to us to be relevant in identifying needs: to discover more about how people and organizations are affected and damaged by their needs; to assess public opinion regarding local community goals and priorities; to scrutinize critically existing development programmes, services and planning.

The relevance of rights language

While needs represent what people perceive as want and deprivation, not all needs justify rights. Nor, of course, is it need alone which creates a right; in addition, there must be a general expectation in society that this need ought to be met. Rights are created when needs have appropriately coalesced with societal expectations, thus establishing *legitimation*.[11]

Unlike traditional resource-led approaches, a needs-led perspective on economic, social and cultural rights starts from the *unmet needs* of the poor. The key is to identify those needs before focusing on the means to meet them.

A concrete example is health. The scope and meaning of the *right to health* as a human right have gradually been clarified as needs; societal expectations concerning the right to health care and the right to health protection have come together.[12] This is characteristic of economic, social and cultural rights in general: when rights are proclaimed in national constitutions or international legal instruments, the language in which the need is expressed in regard to a right changes, and the meaning of that particular right rarely becomes self-evident. The significance and implications of a right enshrined in a bill of rights or a human rights treaty have to be clarified: in everyday life, rights are perceived only gradually. Their core content and implications develop over time through judicial and other forms of interpretation and application to concrete cases, as well as through human rights education and strategies.

The right to health does not in itself mean that international organizations or the national state must guarantee an individual's good health. That is not what is at stake in the context of human rights law. The right to health can be explained as follows:

> Three aspects of the right to health have been enshrined in the international instruments on human rights: the declaration of the right to health as a basic human right; the prescription of standards aimed at meeting the health needs of specific groups of persons; and the prescription of ways and means for implementing the right to health.[13]

While this may be seen as a definition of the core content of the right itself, the question is exactly where the *need* for health care and the *right* to health meet. This became concretely manifest in the Declaration of Alma-Ata, adopted by the World Health Organization (WHO) and UNICEF at an international conference on primary health care in 1978:

> Health, which is a state of complete physical, mental and social well-being, and not merely the absence of disease or infirmity, is a fundamental human right and... the attainment of the highest possible level of health is a most important *world-wide social goal* whose *realization requires the action* of many other social and economic sectors in addition to the health sector [italics added].

This illustrates that needs and rights meet when they are related to explicit *social goals or societal expectations* and thus receive *legitimation* and *require action*. The use of rights language in regard to social goals conveys a specific priority to those goals. Conceptualizing unmet needs for food, water, shelter in terms of rights emphasizes that meeting these needs is a *common good*, a public interest, not just the solution to a developmental or technical "problem". Furthermore, a rights approach offers a vocabulary that advances and encourages the identification of the right holders.

In this sense, human rights can indeed be perceived as legitimation-processes of different needs. Recognizing needs as legitimate and expressing them in human rights terms entails future tasks for human rights, development and peace organizations. The first requirement is to identify the specific conditions and circumstances under which needs may acquire the character of rights. A second is to contribute to the perspective that human rights must remain open and open-ended, innovative and integrative.

This relation of needs to rights does not mean that the poor themselves use the language of human rights to express their felt needs. Rather, they present their needs in forms of expression that come closer to the context of their everyday lives. In the words of Albie Sachs of South Africa:

> The needs of the people extend beyond their material birthright of clean water, medical treatment and food. People want to feel that their pain and their illnesses matter; they want the sense of being an object of concern, of counting, of mattering.[14]

How then can the gap between the lack of substance and meaning of human rights in everyday life and the elite language of human rights law be bridged? How can the category of economic, social and cultural rights become more significant and meaningful for common people? The first task here is to ensure that human rights are in effect the rights of the poor, not an instrument to protect the powerful.

However, this does not imply simply addressing the realities of poverty, displacement and vulnerability in terms of economic, social and cultural rights. It also means linking human rights discourse to *alternative languages of resistance*. There is indeed a tendency to extend the language of rights, but are there not more effective ways to advance the need for health care, food and housing?[15]

Denied needs and the violation of human dignity

There is a gap between the dignity embodied in human rights and what we have described as the "elite language" of law. While the standard of human dignity is of utmost relevance to a needs-orientation, this raises the question of the cultural context in which a violation occurs and the language people use. To borrow an example: When a man slaps a woman in Princeton, she may say, "You violated my *rights*." A woman in Khartoum might say, "You violated my *dignity*." A woman in KwaZulu would say, "You violated *custom*." All three women protest, yet only one speaks in the language of rights.[16]

The contribution which different cultures and traditions can bring to a better comprehension and recognition of human dignity and of the human rights proclaimed by the Universal Declaration is extremely important. Mary Robinson, United Nations High Commissioner for Human Rights, has said in this regard:

> The 50th Anniversary of the Universal Declaration of Human Rights has encouraged people all over the world to reflect on the meaning of the Declaration for them and on the contribution their own civilization and traditions can bring to a better understanding and a fuller realization of the rights proclaimed by the Declaration. This, in my view, is at the heart of the universality of the Declaration. It is a document which each human being can approach from her or his own culture and traditions and which has for everyone a message of human dignity.[17]

Rights language can be activating, symbolic and emotive. In some places, the political culture cannot even be understood apart from an idiom of dignity and rights. In other cultures, however, there is not much substance in the idea of rights. And, as we have seen, in still other cultures the language of rights may even be *obscurantist* – for example, where the right to food or shelter has been recognized, but runs up against the constraints on the country's resources.[18] Efforts to relate rights language to alternative languages of resistance should thus concentrate on contextual diversity.

From this perspective, the language of rights can be particularly useful under conditions of transformation of state and society. A recent example was the debate around the Bill of Rights in the new South African constitution. According to Albie Sachs, this debate took place on two fronts. The first was the confrontation at the public level over economic, social and cultural rights: some supported the inclusion of these rights as a constitutional acknowledgment of their importance; others wanted to restrict the Bill of Rights to certain fundamental freedoms that impose limits on state action. The second front related to the changing nature of the struggle in South Africa. There is an almost hidden debate within the anti-apartheid movement, Sachs says, in which many people have resisted the conversion of a lifelong struggle for power and against repression into a contest for rights.

In this context, Sachs points to the idea of rights to empower people *psychologically*, to strengthen the sense of human dignity, self-determination and self-affirmation, and to instill in people a healthy scepticism about states and political parties. History has shown again and again that those who come to power may subsequently violate others' rights, first of their former oppressors, then of persons in their own ranks. There is fear that without rights language, South Africa would end up with a totally uncaring market system that would not solve any of its problems.[19]

Conclusion

Because of the limited significance of traditional methods of dealing with human rights violations, the question arises of what rights discourse adds to needs and what role a human rights ethos can play in current policies. We have argued that needs can be seen as dynamic sources of social policies. Conceptualizing needs in terms of rights emphasizes the relevance of meeting needs as a social goal. This goal receives priority in terms of the common good or the public interest. This also encourages the identification of the rights-holder and requires further action. Indeed, the participation of individuals and groups in matters which affect themselves is indispensable to the protection of all human rights. Crucial in this regard is that rights concepts represent and imply human dignity. The challenge before us is to clarify further the meaning of a renewed focus on human dignity in the context of human rights.

NOTES

1 Linda Richter, "Many Kinds of Deprivation: Young Children and their Families in South Africa", in Lotty Eldering and Paul Leseman, eds, *Early Intervention and Culture: Preparation for Literacy – The Interface between Theory and Practice*, UNESCO, 1993, pp.95-96.

2 Henry Shue, *Basic Rights, Subsistence, Affluence and US Foreign Policy*, Princeton NJ, Princeton UP, 1980, p.34.

3 Joseph Wronka, *Human Rights and Social Policy in the 21st Century*, pp.23-25.

4 Abraham Maslow, "A Theory of Human Motivation", *Psychological Review*, Vol. 50, 1943, pp.370-96.

5 Linda Richter, *loc. cit.*

6 Cf. David Gil, *Unravelling Social Policy*, Cambridge, Schenkman, 1990, 5th ed., 1992.

7 Cf. James Bradshaw, "The Concept of Need", *New Society*, Vol. 30, 1972, pp.640-43.

8 Len Doyal and Ian Gough, *A Theory of Human Need*, London, Macmillan, 1991, p.1.

9 Cf. Kenneth Pigg, Joe Carrier and Ted McDonland, "Needs Assessment: Uses in Program Planning", presentation to the annual meeting of the American Evaluation Association, Sept. 1995; Jack McKillip, *Needs Analysis: Tools for the Human Services and Education*, Newbury Park, Sage, 1987.

10 Cf. UN Commission on Human Rights, "Question of the realization in all countries of the Economic, Social and Cultural Rights contained in the Universal Declaration of Human Rights and in the International Covenant on Economic, Social and Cultural Rights, and study of special problems which the developing countries face in their efforts to achieve these human rights", Item 5 of the provisional agenda, 54th session, E/CN.4/1998/25, 22 Dec. 1997, no.1.

11 Cf. Joshua Aasgaard, "An Inquiry into Basic Rights: Advancing Rights in the Theories of Lomasky, Shue and Gewirth", master's

54

thesis, Department of Political Science, University of New Orleans, 1993, ch. 4.

[12] Virginia A. Leary, "The Right to Health in International Human Rights Law", *Human Rights*, Vol. 1, No. 1, p.1.

[13] Theo van Boven, in Rene-Jean Dupuy, ed., *The Right to Health as a Human Right*, Alphen aan de Rijn, Sijthoff & Noordhoff, 1979, pp.54-55.

[14] Albie Sachs, in *Economic and Social Rights and the Right to Health*, Cambridge MA, Harvard Law School Human Rights Program, 1995, p.14.

[15] *Ibid.*, pp.5f.

[16] The example comes from Abdullahi An-Na'im, Amy Madigan and Gary Minkley, "Cultural Transformations and Human Rights in Africa: A Preliminary Report", the Law and Religion Program of Emory University School of Law.

[17] Address to a seminar on "Enriching the Universality of Human Rights: Islamic Perspectives on the Universal Declaration of Human Rights", Geneva, Nov. 1998, HR/98/85, 9 Nov. 1998.

[18] Albie Sachs, *op. cit.*, pp.12-13.

[19] *Ibid.*

5. Human Dignity and Humiliation

> It is important to distinguish between having or using a concept and the clear or explicit recognition and elucidation of it... Thus persons might have and use the concept of a right without explicitly having a single word for it.[1]
>
> Alan Gewirth

Human dignity, a core value in most religions, needs to be brought to the centre of the international human rights debate. That is the heart of the argument of this chapter, which seeks to relate dignity and its opposite – humiliation – to fundamental standards for humanity. Regaining the basic notion of dignity is especially critical in a time when *us-them* divides are being revived. In conflicts around ethnic identity, this is often expressed in the belief that others cannot and ought not to share *our* space, that the land belongs to *us*, that *we* determine *our* own destiny.

A renewed focus on human dignity in the context of human rights implies at least three elements. The first is a clear insistence that human dignity provides a *critical standard* or basic norm to judge any person, group, organization, institution or action that denies human equality and freedom and thus humiliates and dehumanizes people. Second, the concept of dignity points to that area of being human in which the *vulnerable* and *fragile* dimensions of existence are recognized to have priority. Third, dignity offers a decisive indicator of the *sustainability* of efforts towards the everyday realization of human rights.[2]

These issues have had a high profile during recent United Nations discussions of "minimum humanitarian standards", both in the Commission on Human Rights and the Sub-Commission on the Prevention of Discrimination and the Protection of Minorities. The point of departure has been the recognition that it is often situations of *internal violence* which pose the greatest threats to human dignity and freedom. Such situations elicit considerable disagreement around questions of applying the norms of both international human rights law and international humanitarian law. For example, at what point does internal violence reach such a level that the rules of international humanitarian law become applicable? In the case of international human rights law, the issue is that some human rights norms are not specific enough to be effective in situations of violent conflict. We shall return to this debate on fundamental standards of human rights law and humanitarian law later in this chapter.

From human development to human dignity

Disintegrating states, internal conflicts and us-them divides may increasingly become the normal context for the work of human rights, development and peace organizations. The UN Development Programme has underscored that human rights cuts across work for peace and security, humanitarian relief and development.[3] For UNDP, "sustainable human development" encompasses all human rights – civil and political; economic, social and cultural; and collective rights. Case-by-case approaches to human rights violations – monitoring, publicizing abuses and holding states accountable for implementation – must be complemented by *active protection and advancement* of human rights. This means that development which seeks to expand choices for all people must also aim at protecting the systems on which all life depends. The problem is that initiatives towards sustainable human development are increasingly confronted with internal conflicts and development-induced displacement, which unleash disruption, impoverishment and disempowerment, making people more vulnerable and destroying community and development efforts.[4]

In such contexts, according to the UNDP policy document, sustainable human development "*aims* to eliminate poverty, and to promote human dignity and rights". It is precisely this notion of "aiming" which creates the problem. Dignity and rights are basic standards and norms, which cannot be approached in terms of an "aim", as the outcome of a process, in the same way as UNDP *aims* at eradicating poverty. Furthermore, strategies for sustainable human development may themselves have as an unintended outcome the violation of people's economic, social and cultural rights – as the term "development-induced displacement" implies.

Focusing on the implementation of economic, social and cultural rights requires a shift *from development to dignity.* This demands further reflection on basic humanitarian standards. While human dignity is indeed related to health, housing, clean water and clean air, education and other social environments and preconditions, it is also a basic standard in itself. In repressive environments, in situations of chaos and barbarity, where sustainable human development and human rights are ruined or destroyed, human dignity is often all that people have left – life's "bottom line". The ground for acting in such situations is *indignation* about humiliation, or recognition and protection of people's dignity. As the preamble to the Universal Declaration of Human Rights puts it: "Recognition of the inherent dignity and of the equal and inalienable rights of all members of the human family is the foundation of freedom, justice and peace in the world."

What is human dignity?

The term human dignity is used extensively in some cultures, but hardly at all in others. Not surprisingly, violations of human dignity are also understood differently. For example, many traditional cultures have viewed death as inherently possessing dignity, so that victims could negate their humiliation through death.[5]

In their well-known pastoral message on "Economic Justice for All" (1986), the US Catholic bishops insisted that human dignity does not come from status, nationality, ethnicity or any human accomplishment. Dignity characterizes each and every person simply because of his or her being human. Hence, dignity is a category of *being*. This point of view is different from the philosophical position that people *have* dignity which cannot be gained or lost. Indeed, no one can take your dignity away from you – not if you are poor, or belong to an ethnic minority, or are physically or mentally disabled. Human existence as such has meaning, even if an individual person is not himself or herself convinced of that.[6] Along the same line, dignity means respect for all other persons, no matter what their capacities or conditions of life.

There are, as Gustavo Gutiérrez has put it, no *no-personas*, no "nobodies".[7] In this sense, addressing the violation of human dignity can be seen as the hard core of strategies to protect human rights.

The "human" element

The notion of human implies that people enjoy dignity as inherent to all human beings and by virtue of their shared humanity. What, then, does the human element mean in regard to *non-human beings* and the dignity of *all living creatures*? In debates on animal rights, for example, different ethical approaches have been developed, which are characterized as either anthropocentrist (anthropo-relational) or non-anthropocentrist (biocentrist). The former approach holds that it is people who attribute dignity to living creatures – recognizing the risks involved in projecting human experiences and ideas. The core element in anthropocentrist ethics is precisely the human capacity for free decision-making and for taking up responsibility. Non-anthropocentrist ethics views dignity as an attribute inherent in all animate species. Seen from this angle, the decisive argument is that the very existence of non-human beings grounds their dignity. This requires fundamental respect for the existence of other beings, regardless of any human meaning or purposes. In the end, the question is whether human beings as such enjoy more dignity than any other living creature.

Dignity, humiliation and human agency

Because the term "human dignity" is so commonly used, we should recognize its different meanings and nuances in different cultures and religions.[8] We begin in this section by focusing on the concept of dignity in political philosophy, starting with its opposite: maltreatment, humiliation and dehumanization.

At least four interrelated forms of maltreatment can be distinguished: causing suffering, restricting freedom, violating rights and perpetrating injustice.[9]

Maltreatment often brings about humiliation. While humiliation has always existed in everyday life, it has never been seen as a central notion in discussions of human rights policies and strategies, where concepts like injustice, inequality, discrimination, non-recognition, marginalization and exclusion have generally prevailed.[10]

The Israeli political philosopher Avishai Margalit relates the idea of humiliation to injury of self-respect: it is "any sort of behaviour or condition that constitutes a sound reason for a person to consider his or her self-respect injured".[11] In Margalit's view, people respect each other on the basis of their autonomy and their ability to be *human agents*, to change, to reshape their lives.[12] Humiliation is thus a form of cruelty which destroys people's capacity to believe in themselves, to take initiatives and to change their own situation. This does not apply only to individuals; the exclusion of groups of people, as in fascism and contemporary forms of religious nationalism and ethnic cleansing, violates their human dignity, humiliates them and is thus a crime against humanity. Humiliation and dehumanization matter so much because of their effects not only on people's fundamental freedoms, but also on their capacity to be agents to change their own situation.

What one person experiences as humiliating may be felt by someone else as maltreatment, embarrassment or dishonour but not as humiliation. How then are we to identify humiliation and vulnerability to it? Which practices and institutions are humiliating? When do we face humiliation? Margalit identifies three different though inter-related senses of the term "humiliation": (1) treating human beings as if they were tools and things, not human, as beasts, machines, subhumans or inferiors; (2) acting in ways that manifest or lead to loss of basic control in other people's lives; (3) rejecting the humanity of a person, in effect excluding a human being from the "Family of Man".[13] Examples are the degradation of people in camps or by colonial regimes; Stalinist invasions of privacy, intimacy and friendship; subjecting people to extreme poverty; or structural violation of human rights.

Margalit elaborates this in terms of systematic institutional humiliation:

> Since we are concerned with institutional humiliation – whose agents are clerks, police, soldiers, prison wardens, teachers, social workers, judges and all the other agents of authority – we can ignore the subjective intentions of the humiliators in examining whether their actions are degrading.[14]

In addressing the elimination of systematic institutional humiliation, Margalit distinguishes a *civilized* society from a *decent* society. A civilized society is one in which individuals do not humiliate each other; a decent society is one whose institutions do not humiliate its members, a society which "fights conditions which constitute a justification for its dependents to consider themselves humiliated."[15] This distinction between a decent and a civilized society is however ambiguous, since the distinction between individual behaviour and institutional behaviour is not always easy to make. Margalit himself argues that some forms of individual humiliation – for example, the way prisoners attack each other – must be regarded as institutional humiliation.

The idea of *human agency* on which Margalit relies appears to be rooted in Immanuel Kant's philosophy. For Kant human dignity is of unique, unconditional and absolute value, and must take precedence in a conflict of any type. Kant saw human dignity as grounded in human autonomy and the capacity of the human being as a moral agent. The unconditional dignity of human beings as rational and moral agents is also expressed in his famous categorical imperative: "act in such a way that you always treat humanity, whether in your own person or in the person of any other, never simply as a means, but always at the same time as an end".[16]

Against this background we see that the notion of human dignity has to do with everyone's basic status as deserving of moral respect, as unconditioned and as an end in itself. *Self-respect* can be seen as the most basic primary good, because without it there is no point in doing anything at all.[17]

Human dignity and transcendence

Most of the world's religions have developed and maintained impressive ethical approaches to human dignity through the ages.[18] What stands out in comparing a political philosophical approach to human dignity, such as that discussed above, with the body of Christian social thought is that for the latter human dignity is prior to individual freedom of choice and human autonomy. Christianity and Judaism ground self-determination and autonomy in the dignity of the human person as image of God (*be-tselem elohim, imago Dei*). Created in the image of God, each individual is worthy of dignity and respect. This link between the *inherent* character of human dignity (dignity as a given) and its *transcendental* origin (dignity as a grace) is of ultimate relevance precisely in those environments where the conditions for free choice are destroyed and people cannot fully exercise their self-determination: in cases of dictatorship, war and disaster, or because of physical or mental disabilities.

This relationship between the inherence and the transcendence of human dignity leads to the insight that the unconditional worth of a human being is not finally derived from his or her capacity for autonomy and self-determination; on the contrary, human dignity is inalienable. This goes far beyond the Kantian approach to human dignity and autonomy which is often more central to human rights debates: the idea that the human "self" and human autonomy are the foundation of morality and the ultimate ground for human rights, without any further external reference.[19]

In theistic religions such as Christianity, Islam and Judaism, human dignity is intrinsically linked to *creation* – to God's revelation and God's creative act – or to the human being as image of God. All of creation has intrinsic value and worth, and is deserving of respect. And because human beings *are* creatures with dignity, they *have* rights. In what follows, we shall explore this further and then link it to notions of dignity in nontheistic religions such as Buddhism.

Dignity in theistic religions

In the history of Christianity, foundations for human dignity can indeed be found in the ideas of the God-likeness of the human being or creation "in the image of God". This concept points to the ambivalent character of human beings. The creation narratives of Genesis 1-3, in which God brings cosmos into being out of chaos (*creatio ex nihilo*), tell on the one hand about Paradise, the prospects of light, happiness and goodness, unity and peace. On the other hand is the account of how the human being injures and destroys life by bringing about evil, disintegration and brokenness. Evil is set forth as part of the inner life of human beings and of the world at large: it attracts, captivates and seduces, so that people mingle with evil, capitulate and surrender, and communicate it to others. The two sides – unity and chaos, good and evil, happiness because of the good and sorrow over the evil – cannot be disconnected; they are part of each other. Because of this intrinsic association, the concept of the human being as the image of God also contains the idea of a unique human destiny towards fulfilment. It is not mere human existence or presence which counts, but that human beings are there with a purpose.

In Christian social thinking, human dignity is a given – an intrinsic part of humanity – and a good. The existence of the human being is of inestimable value. Moreover, the *unique* dignity of each and every individual is also a point of departure in Christian social ethics: for God there are no privileged human beings by birth, status or property. All people have human dignity: the value and worth of each is equal to others. On this basis, all people have the right to a humane existence.[20] In principle this means that each human person is equal to all others in dignity and rights.

Along with their basic rights, each individual and the state have *duties* – obligations to respect the rights of others. On this basis, human dignity can be seen as a *decisive* criterion for humanity. In the tradition of Christian social thought, all other rights are secondary to the basic human dignity of individuals. This is the foundation for adjudicating conflicts over human rights or clashes between one standard or right and another.

In everyday life, human dignity has implications for such issues as property and subsidiarity. Christianity defends the right to *property*, considering the goods one owns as legitimate and necessary, but also insists that private property is always subordinate to social duties, since the goods of the earth serve a universal destination, the common good. The principle of *subsidiarity* protects the existence of smaller units.[21] Major institutions like the state must limit their activities to those that cannot be part of the competence and capacity of smaller units. Larger social units may not interfere with and overrule what can adequately be done by smaller social units, and may not impair their capacities, potentials and means. Hence the state has the responsibility and the duty to respect, protect and support smaller social units and associations. The principle of subsidiarity also limits active interventions in everyday life of individual people by international bodies, states and major social associations.[22]

Theistic religions like Judaism and Islam appear to express themselves more in terms of *duties* than rights. In fact, in classical Hebrew texts there is no real equivalent to the term "rights", although there are many counterparts to the term "duty" – such as "commandments" (*mitsvot*) and "obligations" (*hovot*).

In recent decades, various Islamic organizations have formulated declarations of human rights, giving priority to the Qur'an and to Shar'ia (Islamic law). For example, the 1990 Cairo Declaration of Human Rights states that "all rights and freedoms mentioned in this statement are subject to the Islamic Shar'ia" (Article 24), adding that "the Islamic Shar'ia is the only source for the interpretation or explanation of each individual article" (Article 25). At the same time, Islam confesses the oneness of God, which entails the concept of the oneness of humanity; and it has laid down some universal fundamental rights for humanity, which are to be observed and respected under all circumstances. This means that Islam in principle does not restrict human rights to the geographical limits of its own state. It is also not permissible to oppress women, children, old people, the sick or the wounded. The hungry person must be fed, the naked clothed and the diseased treated.[23] Furthermore, human rights in Islam have been granted by God, not by any legislative gathering. Though human beings can become "the lowest of the lowest", the Qur'an declares that they have been made "in the best of moulds", having the ability to think, the knowledge of right and wrong, and the obligation to do good and to avoid evil.

Dignity in non-theistic religions (Buddhism)

Is the notion of human dignity in Buddhism entirely the product of an alien cultural tradition? Do human rights have a place on the Buddhist agenda? Can they be grounded in Buddhist religion? On the face of it, the idea of "human dignity" as the source of human rights does sound alien in a context which includes teachings such as "no-self". Damien Keown suggests that the foundation and justification for human rights in various forms of Buddhism can be found more in the interrelatedness of beings or in the dynamic nature of relationships than in the human nature of persons themselves.[24] Rights are present in terms of what is "due" in reciprocal relationships among and between individuals. What is due in any situation is determined by reference to *dharma*, which determines what is right and just in all contexts and from all perspectives. Although the requirements of *dharma* are expressed in the form of duties rather than rights, Keown says it would be going too far to maintain that the term "rights" is alien to Buddhism. One of the most fruitful approaches to rights in Buddhism seems to be one which links the human element to the "good-in-community", "which locates human rights and dignity within a comprehensive account of *human goodness*, and which sees basic rights and freedoms as integrally related to human flourishing and self-realization".[25]

Dignity, rights and fundamental standards of humanity

Humanity is not something external to a person but embraces and constitutes a person's whole life. The equal dignity of every human being is the principle on which the *universality* of human rights is founded. The Universal Declaration of Human Rights and the two International Covenants link dignity immediately with *equality*; in other words, respect for and protection of their dignity is a right that belongs to each and every person.[26] Human dignity is a unique, universal and normative concept, which is both protected by law and at the same time a basic norm and standard in law. This implies that rights are not granted to human beings but are *intrinsically* part of their humanity.

The concept of right

The English term "right" is derived from the Latin *rectus*, straight, which in turn can be traced to the Greek *orektos*, stretched out or upright – as opposed to crooked, twisted and bent. Both the English and Latin words have a more distant ancestor in the Sanskrit *rju*, straight or upright, and the Pali *uju* (or *ujju*), straight, direct, straightforward, honest, upright.[27]

In the history of the West, the notion of straightness came to be extended from the physical to the ethical realm: from *rectus* to rectitude. A next step, within the moral domain, was that right came to be associated with a personal *entitlement* of some kind: a shift in emphasis from doing something *because it is right*, to doing something because one *has a right* to do it.[28] This is a qualitative change: there is no word in the original Sanskrit or Pali which conveys the idea of a right or rights as a subjective entitlement. Thomas Aquinas in the 13th century, as well as Suarez, Grotius and Hobbes in the 17th century, exercised a strong influence in this direction. Towards the end of the 17th century, the English philosopher John Locke gave prominence to the concept of *natural rights* – those which flow from human *nature*.

As noted in the comment by Alan Gewirth cited at the head of this chapter, however, the concept of rights may exist even where there is no single specific term for expressing it.

In short, the modern vocabulary and grammar of rights is a many-faceted instrument for reporting and asserting the requirements or other implications of a relationship of justice from the point of view of the person(s) who benefit(s) from that relationship. It provides a way of talking about "what is just" from a special angle: the viewpoint of the "other(s)" to whom something (including, *inter alia*, freedom of choice) is owed or due, and who would be wronged if denied that something.[29]

Finnis goes on to observe that African tribal regimes of law have shown that terms like "right" and "duty" are connected to words like *ought* or *due*, because "'due' looks both ways along a juridical relationship, both to what one is due to do, and to what is due to one".[30]

Fundamental standards of humanity

As we said at the beginning of this chapter, the gap between the gross abuses of human rights perpetrated in situations of internal violence and an evident lack of clear rules covering such situations in international law has motivated recent efforts to articulate fundamental standards of humanity. A point of departure was the elaboration by a group of non-governmental experts of a Declaration on Minimum Humanitarian Standards in Turku, Finland, in 1990. After study by the Sub-Commission on Prevention of Discrimination and Protection of Minorities in 1991 and 1994, this Declaration was transmitted to the UN Commission on Human Rights. Following a workshop in Cape Town in September 1996, the Commission on Human Rights requested the Secretary-General of the UN Economic and Social Council to prepare an analytical report on the issue of fundamental standards of humanity.

What is noteworthy in the course of this discussion of fundamental humanitarian standards is the importance given to addressing the root causes of violence and conflict. In the context of human rights abuses and the "us-them" divide in episodes of internal violence, fundamental standards of humanity must be identified because existing human rights law does not adequately address these particular situations. Discussion has focused both on the gaps in the protection provided by humanitarian law and on the inadequacies and lack of specificity of existing standards of human rights law. For example, groups such as militias, which are not part of the state's armed forces, are in a strict sense not legally bound by international human rights treaties, which are instruments adopted by states and formally ratified only by states. Moreover, the supervisory mechanisms established by these treaties are not mandated to monitor or take action on the activities of armed groups.[31] The point here is that when an armed group within a country is killing people or expelling them from their homes, humiliating and dehumanizing them, engaging in acts of terror or indiscriminate violence, an issue of potential international concern is raised, especially if the government of the country has lost control.[32] But international intervention in such situations is precarious: human rights means in the first place holding governments accountable to common standards. This poses a dilemma: how can this human rights achievement be sustained at an international scale while ensuring at the same time that human rights are significant and relevant in internal conflicts?

This is why a statement on fundamental standards of humanity, setting out basic principles of human rights and humanitarian law in situations of internal violence, is seen as beneficial and even necessary. While these two branches of law operate in distinct spheres, internal violence and conflict bring them together. From the perspective of economic, social and cultural rights, the central issue is addressing basic needs, especially of people faced with poverty, displacement and vulnerability, which become more acute in such situations. In other words, some basic guarantees are required in all circumstances, irrespective of the legal characterization of the situation and whether or not a state of public emergency has been officially proclaimed. Limiting the scope of application of such fundamental standards would create contradictions and disparities.

The "us-them" divide: an intercultural perspective

The concept of dignity as a fundamental standard of humanity appears to be very relevant in relation to the *us-*

them divide which is so manifest in the context of nationalism and extremism. However, the very dignity which may serve as cultural support for struggles by oppressed minorities may at the same time be invoked to justify ethnic cleansing.[33] A group may even think it is acting in the interest of true humanity by purifying the world of others whom they consider to be pseudo- or sub-human. In such contexts, dignity becomes a slippery concept, susceptible to misuse and abuse by all kinds of power-seekers.

In the context of human rights the fundamental standard of human dignity may contribute to the development of an *inter*-cultural perspective, which recognizes the value of dignity related to the substance of rights in different cultural contexts. Indeed, the focus and objectives we have been discussing require an innovation that can break through the paralyzing impasse of the *universalism-relativism* debate. A *trans*-cultural perspective, which claims that the formulations in the Universal Declaration of Human Rights are so fundamental that no divergence is possible, is far removed from the concrete realities of many local and regional contexts. An *intra*-cultural perspective, on the other hand, identifies the genesis of human rights within a specific context, thus limiting their validity and relevance to that particular culture, its local customs and traditions. What we are proposing is rather an *inter*-cultural perspective, which recognizes the presence and substance of human rights in different social, cultural and religious contexts, and links local practices and formulations of rights to internationally and nationally enshrined human rights frameworks and mechanisms for implementation.

Conclusion

Human dignity is what brings respect and recognition. The protection of human dignity as the basic source and fundamental standard of human rights seems often to be a forgotten element in the international human rights debate, quickly cited as a point of departure and then left aside. Thus in this chapter we have set out the need to shift the focus in the human rights debate from development towards basic human dignity. Human dignity can create a protective domain for vital human preoccupations without denying the fragility of life and the vulnerability of communities. Human rights discourse, which is often legalistic and elitist, needs to be confronted with its roots.

We have shown that, despite diversities of terminology, notions of dignity and rights are present in and compatible with different religious and cultural traditions. This does not of course mean that the realization of human dignity in society is automatic; it is violated grossly and systematically. In every society, community and organization, the practice of realizing human dignity is a complex process. Human dignity requires *concerted actions* against violations in order to achieve structural enjoyment of economic, social and cultural rights. A major resource for such actions is people's perceptions and worldviews, their cultures and religions.

How can human dignity be restored and supported when it is denied, violated or contradicted? Human rights approaches encourage a more humane and meaningful life. Human rights embody values and meanings which are in fact not so "common" in everyday life. By stimulating the desire for a good life, they offer a counter-story to the events and processes of everyday reality. They suggest broader perspectives, extension of capabilities, an open-ended language, the possibility of speaking out, providing meaning and resources for a dignified life.

From an inter-cultural perspective, the notion of human dignity cannot simply be imposed on cultures where it is not self-evident. Restraint and caution are needed. When human dignity is brought to the centre of international debate, it must be recognized that dignity is meaningful only if it corresponds to the specific identity, including language, of a particular culture. In such an inter-cultural perspective, dignity may indeed become the foundation for a humane, good and meaningful life.

70

NOTES

1 Quoted in Richard Dagger, "Rights", in Terence Ball et al., eds, *Political Innovation and Conceptual Change*, Cambridge, Cambridge UP, 1989, p.286.

2 On the idea of the sustainability of social change, see Hans Opschoor, "Development and Sustainability in a Globalizing World", unpublished paper for an ISS-SID conference, The Hague, 10 June 1998, p.4.

3 Cf. the 1998 UNDP policy document *Integrating Human Rights with Sustainable Human Development*.

4 On development-induced displacement, see also Ranjit Dwivedi, "Displacement, Risks and Resistance: Local Perceptions and Actions in the Sardar Sarovar", *Development and Change*, Vol. 30, No. 1, 1999, pp.43-45.

5 See Avishai Margalit and Gabriel Motzkin, "The Uniqueness of the Holocaust", *Philosophy and Public Affairs*, Vol. 25, No. 1, 1996.

6 Matthijs de Blois, "Self-Determination or Human Dignity: The Core Principle of Human Rights", in Mielle Bulterman, Aart Hendriks and Jacqueline Smith, eds, *To Baehr in Our Minds: Essays on Human Rights from the Heart of the Netherlands*, Utrecht, Netherlands Institute of Human Rights, 1998, p.531.

7 Gustavo Gutiérrez, *La Fuerza Histórica de los Pobres*, Salamanca, Sígueme, 1982, p.248. See also Jacques Van Nieuwenhove, *Bronnen van Bevrijding: Varianten in de Theologie van Gustavo Gutiérrez*, Kampen, Kok, 1991, p.102.

8 See Alan Gewirth, "Human Dignity as the Basis of Rights", in Michael Meyer and W.A. Parent, eds, *The Construction of Rights: Human Dignity and American Values*, Ithaca, Cornell UP, 1992, pp.10-28; Rubin Gotesky and Ervin Laszlo, eds, *Human Dignity*, New York, Gordon & Breach, 1970.

9 Steven Lukes, "Humiliation and the Politics of Identity", *Social Research*, Vol. 64, No. 1, 1997, pp.36-52; Frederic Schick, "On Humiliation", *ibid.*, pp.131-47.

10 See also Berma Klein Goldewijk and Ben Schennink, *Liberation from Exclusion: Proceedings of a Conference on Liberation from Below in Latin America and Eastern Europe*, Nijmegen, Peace Research Centre, 1993, pp.213-27.

11 Avishai Margalit, *The Decent Society*, Cambridge MA, Harvard UP, 1996, p.9.

12 *Ibid.*, p.70.

13 *Ibid.*, p.108; cf. pp.121,144,146. See also Steven Lukes, *loc. cit.*

14 Margalit, *op. cit.*, p.128.

15 *Ibid.*, p.10.

16 Gewirth says that "the necessary attribution of inherent dignity to all human beings is dialectically established, for all humans are actual, prospective, or potential agents"; "Human Dignity as the Basis of Rights", *loc. cit.*, p.23.

[17] For a more elaborated approach to "dignity" see Berma Klein Gold-ewijk, *The Quest for Human Dignity: Religion and Human Rights in a Context of Globalization and Conflict*, States and Societies Paper No. 98-17, The Hague, Institute of Social Studies, 1998.

[18] Cf. Jacques Van Nieuwenhove and Berma Klein Goldewijk, eds, *Popular Religion, Liberation and Contextual Theology*, Kampen, Kok, 1991.

[19] Matthijs de Blois, "Self-Determination or Human Dignity", *loc. cit.*, p.524.

[20] For this theme in Catholic social thought, see for example Pius XI, *Quadragesimo Anno* (1931), para. 136; John XXIII, *Mater et Magistra* (1961), para. 110, and *Pacem in Terris* (1963), paras 35, 38, 41; see also *Gaudium et Spes* (1965), paras 12-22.

[21] Cf. Pius XI, *Quadragesimo Anno*, para. 79; John XXIII broadens the principle of subsidiarity towards more just relationships as part of the international order; *Mater et Magistra*, paras 169-70.

[22] Cf. Congregation for the Doctrine of the Faith, *Donum Vitae*, 1987, ch. 3.

[23] Cf. Abdullahi Ahmed An-Na'im, "Toward an Islamic Hermeneutics for Human Rights", in Abdullahi A. An-Na'im, Jerald D. Gort, Henry Jansen and Hendrik M. Vroom, eds, *Human Rights and Religious Values: An Uneasy Relationship?*, Amsterdam, Rodopi, 1995, pp.229-42.

[24] Damien Keown, "Are There 'Human Rights' in Buddhism?", *Journal of Buddhist Ethics*, Vol. 2, 1995, p.18. On this question see also Masao Abe, "The Buddhist View of Human Rights", in An-Na'im, Gort, Jansen and Vroom, *op. cit.*, pp.144-53; and Kenneth Inada, "A Buddhist Response to the Nature of Human Rights", in Claude E. Welch and Virginia Leary, eds, *Asian Perspectives on Human Rights*, Boulder CO, Westview, 1990, pp.91-103.

[25] Damien Keown, *loc. cit.*, p.22 (italics added).

[26] Cf. Rhoda Howard M. and Jack Donnelly, "Human Dignity, Human Rights and Political Regimes", *American Political Science Review*, Vol. 80, No. 3, Sept. 1986, p.803.

[27] Damien Keown, *loc. cit.*, pp.7,11; see also Jack Donnelly, *The Concept of Human Rights*, London and Sydney, Croom Helm, 1985; Rhoda Howard, "Is There an African Concept of Human Rights?", in R.J. Vincent, ed., *Foreign Policy and Human Rights*, Cambridge, Cambridge UP, 1986, pp.11-32; James C. Hsiung, *Human Rights in East Asia: A Cultural Perspective*, New York, Paragon House, 1985.

[28] Richard Dagger, "Rights", in Terence Ball et al., eds, *Political Innovation and Conceptual Change*, Cambridge, Cambridge UP, 1989, pp.293-94.

[29] J.M. Finnis, *Natural Law and Natural Rights*, Oxford, Clarendon Press, 1980, p.205.

[30] *Ibid.*, p.209.

[31] *Minimum Humanitarian Standards*, analytical report of the secretary-general submitted pursuant to the Commission on Human Rights, Res-

olution 1997/21; document: General, E/CN.4/1998/87, 5 Jan. 1998, no. 59.

[32] *Ibid.*, no.64.

[33] Cf. Glyn Morgan, "The Morality of Nationalism", in *American Political Science Review*, Vol. 92, No. 2, pp.446-47.

6. Identities, Violence and Conflict

Any attempt to exclude a part of humanity from the status of being human is not only an act of injustice but merits the name "crime against humanity". Indeed, the confrontation between different identities is a litmus test for dignity and justice. What is crucial is people's *right to be there* by the very fact of their humanity. This chapter seeks to deepen insights into the dynamics of culture and religion, globalization and violence arising from armed conflicts, which these days are more often internal and civil than international.

Internal conflicts, external aggression, social and economic injustices, ethnic tensions and environmental degradation are among the root causes of large-scale forced population displacements.[1] Human rights abuses associated with these circumstances include the neglect of the rights to food, housing, work, education and health. Situations of internal violence are often accompanied by a breakdown in public institutions: schools are closed, local governments cannot function, police and judicial institutions are out of control.[2] Homes and hospitals, religious and cultural buildings are deliberately destroyed, as are personal belongings and livestock. The life and livelihood of the civilian population, particularly children, is immediately affected.

In the context of the us-them divide, violence is justified by attributing human dignity to *us* but not to *them*. Thus the struggle of people to preserve, protect or stabilize their identity when it appears to be negated, relativized and marginalized is an understandable response to the pressures they must cope with. People concerned with identity and community often pose a greater challenge to political institutions and national boundaries than economic processes and outcomes.[3] In this context of *identity politics*, affirming the dignity of one's own people is too easily transformed into proclaiming "our" superiority and consequently denying the claims and needs of "them".

This chapter explores these issues from a civilizational perspective, relating them to the challenge of finding new strategies to implement economic, social and cultural rights.

Cultural and religious identity, conflict and civil strife

The quest for economic and political integration through globalization has not prevented war or impeded civil conflict. Poverty and inequality have become more widespread, and states have begun to disintegrate under the tensions and conflicts which globalization promotes among nationalities, ethnic groups and religious communities. Conflicts over competing identities, related to territorial claims and the desire for political power, have become a major issue on the contemporary international agenda.

It should be noted that social conflict is not inherently a bad thing: in some contexts, civil strife can create opportunities for beneficial change promoting human rights, redistribution of land and wealth, good governance, justice and sustainable peace. Nor is competition for resources, political participation and cultural identity entirely illegitimate. Indeed, the scarcity of resources such as water, forests and fertile land and imbalances in their allocation particularly affect poor countries. Thus the problem is not so much one of eradicating conflict or eliminating competition as of the limitation of violence.

The classic sociological idea of "collective identity" reflects the "we-ness" of a group in terms of its consolidating around common "essential" characteristics which all members share and internalize – as if these natural attributes were qualities emerging from physiological traits, psychological predispositions or regional features. This approach seems less viable than recognizing that identities are socially constructed.[4] In this sense, ethnicity in itself is not a cause of violent conflict. The fear of some ethnic groups that they may be assimilated into a dominant culture or into a state that is failing and falling apart underlies much of today's identity politics. Other ethnic groups may fear for their physical safety, or for the survival and integrity of their religious and cultural identity. When such insecurities emerge, and the state can no longer arbitrate between groups or provide convincing forms of protection, conflict may explode into violence.

What is and what is not a conflict situation is less clear today than in the past. Conflicts involving ethnic, clan, religious, national or international identities interplay with far-reaching economic, ecological, technological and social changes, often in the context of the erosion of state authority. Their roots lie not in factors like scarcity of resources, border disputes or political failure, but in deeper realities such as humiliation, imposed inequalities, exclusion, vulnerability and fragility.

The vulnerability of peace

The most promising and sustainable policy approach to identity conflicts in ethnically diverse societies seems to be the promotion of *civic identity*: cultural autonomy and security for minorities, including multi-lingualism, and their adequate representation in civil institutions. This of course presupposes that the state does not regard homogeneity as the essence of nationhood or seek to freeze identities (as in apartheid and caste-systems). Nation-building through ethnic homogenization has rarely been successful; domination by one ethnic group provides no long-term stability. Civic identity is rooted in shared values and a common interest in the well-being of all. This implies both a state which considers citizenship central to the relations between individual and nation, and a political society in which stronger communities share resources with the weaker. This requires intense cultural change, socialization and an ethos of the common good, both in public institutions and civil society at large.

Against this background, aiming at a *civilizational perspective*, in which minorities and excluded people can publicly articulate their concerns and assert their cultural identities, may help to overcome the misleading separation between civil and political rights on the one hand and economic, social and cultural rights on the other.[5]

In conflict situations, people's need for a recognized cultural identity and for belonging to a certain territory must be explicitly linked to their place in the wider world and to the coexistence at least of diverse identities. Notions like "cultural identity" have to be reformulated in such a way that people can say *both "us" and "them"*. This may contribute to a political consensus in conformity with the universality of human rights.

The new types of identity conflicts have serious implications for peace. Sadako Ogata, the United Nations High Commissioner for Refugees, has observed how the "fragile peace" of today differs from the more stable peace treaties of the past.[6] The struggles of Croats and Serbs, Hutus and Tutsis, Protestants and Catholics in Northern Ireland, Palestinians and Israelis, Tamils and Sinhalese in Sri Lanka call for a renewed affirmation of peace in a civilizational perspective, linked to a standard of human dignity. The basis and condition for an affirmation of non-discrimination, co-existence, equal rights and peace might be *citizenship* for all those participating in a nation or a territory, rather than *identity*, which is exclusively derived from membership of an ethnic or religious group. In this sense, citizenship is a practical matter of people of different cultural and religious traditions associating and acting together in key institutions of society to improve civic life.

Human rights organizations have not generally given priority to the stability of states and resistance to their disintegration. Indeed, oppressive regimes often condemn human rights actions precisely as threats to the stability of the state. The partial or complete disintegration of states can take many forms, as a result of revolutionary or ethnic wars, mass killings and genocide, disruptive political changes, growing irrelevance in the face of the globalization of the world economy. In whatever form and to whatever extent, state disintegration involves loss of control by state authorities, which leads to economic collapse, civil strife and massive human rights violations. Challenged by social chaos, states may react in repressive ways.

The rapid change or collapse of a state confronts human rights organizations with immense challenges in protecting the most vulnerable from the life-threatening aspects of the situation. When powers which once resided with the state are dispersed in tribes, clans or multinational enterprises, the focus of human rights work is often on human security. In other cases the central need is to strengthen the capacity of civil society to resist the "us-them" divide and promote justice and the public interest (the common good) as necessary for sustainable, peaceful change.[7] Where civil war has become the predominant face of disintegration and internal conflict, civil society strategies appear to be more important. In our opinion, citizenship must be related to structural social and political change, which also includes people's need for cultural belonging and the affirmation of their identity. Shared cultural values, principles and orientations are indispensable for civil society; this in turn implies an intercultural perspective.[8]

Disintegrating states challenge the international human rights movement with the dilemma between the need to support the stability and integrative capacity of states and the need to strengthen the autonomous capacity of civil society. On the one hand, the instability of a state may be the source of massive violations of human rights; on the other hand, its complete breakdown always appears to be a catastrophe. Seen from the angle of this dilemma, religion plays an important role.

Religion and conflict

While acknowledging that neither sociology, anthropology and history of religion nor theology offers a definition of religion which is more than tentative and incomplete, we use the term here to refer to a complex set of beliefs, practices and institutions dealing with the sacred, the mystery, God. Religion offers guidance for conduct in both public and private life amid changing cultures and life-styles; thus it both influences and assimilates characteristics of the culture it is associated with. Spirituality we understand to be a faith commitment that is not necessarily linked to particular religious traditions or institutions.

The relationship between religion in this sense and conflict is inherently ambiguous. Religions may generate conflicts, but they may also contribute to their resolution. They may justify, motivate or even mandate war and violence, but they also require tolerance, peace and global co-existence. Sometimes, religious groups attack each other, or religious leaders issue bellicose statements which are totally incompatible with the teachings and values of their own traditions.[9] The dilemma here is whether religion's place in the public realm should be minimized, because its manipulation fuels conflicts, or strengthened, because it is a possible resource for resolving conflicts.

This dilemma became apparent during the process of drafting the Universal Declaration of Human Rights. The United Nations deliberately dissociated itself from religion: the Universal Declaration does not acknowledge religion as a *source* of human rights.[10] After two devastating world wars, the UN apparently wanted to distance itself from any sort of identification with religion, which had so much contributed to divisiveness and conflict. Already in 1945 the UN Charter had placed religion alongside race, sex and language, and required all nations to promote human rights without distinction as to these four. The Universal Declaration of Human Rights and the subsequent International Covenants follow this approach, but add freedom of thought and conscience as further conditions which may not be made the basis of discrimination.

In situations of internal conflict, it is extremely difficult to separate out specifically religious motivations and factors from the political, cultural or ethnic elements behind the strife. Most studies suggest that cases in which religion is the *principal cause* of violent conflict are extremely rare; the basis is far more commonly economic, political and ideological factors. David Little of the US Institute of Peace identifies three contemporary internal conflicts in which religious factors are central: Sri Lanka (Sinhalese Buddhists versus Tamil Hindu); Sudan (Muslim versus Christian); and Ukraine (Russian Orthodox versus Independent Orthodox versus Roman Catholic). During the conflict in Bosnia, leaders of the Islamic, Roman Catholic and Serbian Orthodox communities there declared that "the characterization of this tragic conflict as a religious war and the misuse of all religious symbols used with the aim to further hatred, must be proscribed and is condemned".[11] Nevertheless, the religious dimension of violent conflicts should not be downplayed. The apartheid regime in South Africa and the forces promoting ethnic cleansing in the former Yugoslavia certainly manipulated believers, appropriated religious resources and falsified religious messages for their own ends. Furthermore, most contemporary violent *intra*-state conflicts do reflect a religious dimension – the conflicts involving Hindus and Muslims in India, the clashes between different branches of Islam in Iraq or Syria, the tensions between Christians and Muslims in Nigeria. Religious issues also justify or fuel many *inter*-state conflicts, such as those between Pakistan and India over Kashmir, between Iran and Iraq, between Israel and the Arab states.[12]

But the *explanatory value* of religious and cultural factors in a violent conflict is often limited. Of course, in the midst of extreme nationalism and ethnic cleansing, your survival might depend on whether you are Muslim, Orthodox or Catholic. But in such a context these terms have lost their religious meaning and are reduced to another way of describing cultural, ethnic or national differences.[13]

Conflicts seem to alter the roles which religious beliefs, practices and institutions play in society. In such situations religious traditions reinterpret and manipulate their justifications for the use of arms — such as *jihad* in Islam or "just war" in the Christian tradition. At the same time, religions redefine themselves in a world of rapid change and increasing tension by taking up or rejecting the values of an emerging global culture.[14] This has led to a growing recognition among political scientists of the consequences of ignoring religion in analyses of poverty, vulnerability, internal conflict and civil strife. Religion and culture are acknowledged as highly significant aspects of global and social change, whose neglect can lead to "uninformed and potentially damaging foreign policy choices".[15] Secularist and functionalist misperceptions in the field of religious and cultural studies, which have led to stereotypes and prejudices about religion as something only for "traditional" and not "modern" people, and thus a marginal and declining force, are being overcome in the light of contemporary international developments.

In the light of this growing recognition of the relevance of religion in international relations, does the religious factor also have to be explicitly integrated into future policy-making? Some scholars hold that an "either-or" approach (conflict mediation on either a religious or a secular basis) must be replaced by a "both-and" perspective.[16] Indeed, it has become evident that identity-based conflicts are resistant to conventional international diplomatic techniques. Reducing the complexities of society to political problems which are amenable to political reforms – or to economic obstacles which can be overcome by economic or social engineering – ignores the fact that "religion is an intractable force that can be quite unresponsive to all the normal instrumentalities of state power and foreign policy".[17]

Violence as a warning that comes too late

Violent conflict has an increasing impact on the health and food security of populations. Alex de Waal notes that food shortages may not simply be the by-product of violent conflict but are often deliberately created as a weapon of war.[18] Violent conflict also directly and indirectly affects health systems. In other words, it exacerbates pre-existing structural weaknesses.[19] Economic, social and cultural changes are thus both at the root of violent conflict and are accelerated by it.

Increasingly, internal conflict and the disintegration of states may become the typical working environment for development cooperation. The abuse of human rights has become a crucial motive for humanitarian intervention to prevent forced displacement of people in internal conflict. Humanitarian aid, which is based on the principles of impartiality, neutrality and independence, focuses on the immediate and the efficient: how to support and protect people's rights in increasingly violent situations. This poses other difficult questions: Does relief aid intensify violent conflict? Is humanitarian aid undermining long-term development?

The fundamental moral and legal aspect of violence is coercion: the use of force or the threat of force *against* the will of another. This points again to the myth of "us" versus "them". The basic resort to violence relates to three different elements: the desire to incapacitate the other so as to impose one's own goals; the urge for aggression because of frustration or revenge for violence suffered now or in the past; and the quest for honour and glory.[20] In this connection, we may distinguish between *violent cultures* that legitimize violence (like machismo), *violent structures* that exploit, repress and alienate people; and *violent actors*, attracted to violence to gain power or to build their own identity over against other groups. Violence has its own distinct logic, which often makes conflict almost intractable. Hence, cultural and structural forms of violence may be as bad as or worse than direct or intimate forms of violence.

There are different ways of terminating violence. The resort to counter-violence as a means to overcome injustice may often in fact be a distraction from the root causes of conflict. The traditional approach of negotiation, pointing out that in the long run all parties lose because of the spiralling violence, may tempt the parties to treat the negotiating table as a verbal battlefield and produce a flat compromise that satisfies no one and does not really move the underlying situation forward. After the negotiation process ends, the relief that the violence is over may blind people to its invisible, long-lasting consequences – trauma and the desire for revenge. Cultures, structures and actors may in fact have become *more* violent, even if this is not immediately expressed. The task remaining may be more difficult and more complex than before the violence.[21]

These limitations point to the need for a strategy that goes beyond violence to the roots of conflict. Such an approach has been developed by Johan Galtung.

A strategy to transform conflict

Galtung has described his concept and strategy as "conflict transformation" in situations of violence.[22] Its point of departure is the thesis that what leads to violence is precisely the *failure to transform conflicts.* Although Galtung does not present and elaborate this approach with a specific reference to human rights, we believe that this strategy can be adapted to the promotion of economic, social and cultural rights in conflict situations.

The starting point of conflict transformation is a recognition that a "meta-conflict logic", as Galtung calls it – the resort to violence, war, physical, verbal or legal power – is often used to decide a "root conflict", which is present *before* violence breaks out. To *transform* the conflict means to change this meta-conflict logic into a new reality by lifting it out of the context in which the parties live it. The transformation consists precisely of adding parties and goals of which the participants themselves have not always thought, thus going beyond the focus on direct violence to structural and cultural violence. In that sense, this strategy introduces a new approach, a new landscape, a new type of reality by making visible and palpable something that has always been present.

Adapting the strategy of conflict transformation to the promotion of economic, social and cultural rights means a shift from direct and often violent conflicts over housing, education or cultural identity towards the root conflicts, which are like basic wounds left unattended when violence explodes. Addressing this root conflict has to do with finding some outcome, exit, transformation. This would include (1) *reconstruction*, rehabilitating the wounded; (2) *restructuring*, rebuilding and reparation after material damage; (3) *reconciliation*, to solve the meta-conflict; and (4) *re-culturing*, to deal with the original, underlying conflicts.

An illustration of the potential of conflict transformation can be found in the Interface Project in Belfast, Northern Ireland, one of the initiatives in the World Council of Churches' Peace to the City Campaign:

The Belfast Interface Project promotes a community development approach to support work carried out by interface communities. An interface is a boundary line between a predominantly Protestant area and a predominantly Catholic area of housing. It can be a solid brick wall, 20 feet high, a steel fence or a road. It may not even be noticeable to others, but local people know exactly where it is. It can be crossed simply by crossing a street, passing a landmark, or turning a corner. There are at least 17 purpose-built "peace-lines", for example walls and fences, between Protestant and Catholic areas. Yet, there are many more "invisible" interfaces between communities in Belfast and other communities in Northern Ireland. North Belfast, especially, is a patchwork quilt of interface communities...

Protestants and Catholics live in separate areas because they feel safer that way or have little choice, so there are lots of interfaces between these communities – particularly in lower-income districts. There are at least three different kinds of interface:

– the "enclave" area, totally surrounded by the "other" community;
– the "split", a wall or boundary evenly separates the two communities;
– the "buffer zone", a mixed community separates two different segregated communities...

Interfaces provide physical protection from inter-community violence, especially for those living furthest away from the interface, and they mark "safe" boundaries so that people know where it is secure to go and where it is not. Interfaces also provide psychological security: a community on one "side" or the other will be made up of people who share roughly the same religious and political outlook and help to create a strong feeling of community identity and solidarity.

Interface communities typically experience an unusual combination of three kinds of disadvantage: (a) high rates of social and economic disadvantage; (b) high levels of ongoing inter-community violence across the interface, especially from young people who are drawn to the interface, often from further afield, and are socialized into inter-community violence there; (c) restricted access to facilities and services "on the other side", like jobs, shops, leisure facilities and social services. This is especially severe in "enclave" areas.

Interface communities have been among those most affected by "the troubles" of the past 30 years. Peace and stability at the interface and the absence of this are both a "barometer" of the health of the society and a key influencing factor in shaping that society.[23]

The Belfast Interface Project aims to transform conflict by promoting community development which supports the work carried out by interface communities through lobbying and challenging policy-makers, assisting development work, disseminating information, encouraging networking and cooperation, and sharing effective practices.

The changing nature of conflict expands the part which can be played by citizens outside government. More evidence is appearing about the positive role religion can play in promoting peace, development and democracy. Religion can motivate people to become deeply involved and strongly committed to stop war and conflict. In some contexts a growing cadre of religious figures and spiritually inspired people in civil society are promoting peaceful change by way of mediation and conflict-resolution, whether in anonymous, behind-the-scenes diplomacy or in more public roles. Shared spiritual convictions or religious values can motivate conflicting parties "to operate on a higher level of trust".[24]

Conclusion

Identity-based conflicts call for new perspectives on economic, social and cultural rights which focus less on state power and more on cultural diversity and the future of humankind. Religion is of considerable importance in introducing civilizational perspectives and processes of social integration. In some contexts religion has become a unifying force for peace-making, while strengthening possibilities for conflict transformation. By helping people to come to grips with displacement and the effects of drastic social change, religions are among the resources for new identity-formation and new social and cultural orientations.

With the changing nature of conflicts, the role played by religiously motivated citizens in conflict mediation and conflict transformation cannot be ignored, for conflict transformation is not primarily political or economic.

NOTES

[1] Cf. *Human Rights and Mass Exoduses,* report of the UN High Commissioner for Human Rights, E/CN.4/1998/51, 30 Jan. 1998, para. 1.

[2] On this see further *Minimum Humanitarian Standards*, analytical report of the Secretary-General, UN Commission on Human Rights, 54th session; General, E/CN.4/1998/87, 5 Jan. 1998.

[3] Cf. John Langan, "Nationalism, Ethnic Conflict and Religion", *Theological Studies*, Vol. 56, No. 1, pp.122-37.

[4] See Karen A. Cerulo, "Identity Construction: New Issues, New Directions", *Annual Review of Sociology*, Vol. 23, 1997, pp.385-410.

[5] Berma Klein Goldewijk and Bas de Gaay Fortman, "Globalization and Civilizational Change: Contemporary Challenges for Religious Response", *Studies in Interreligious Dialogue*, Vol. 8, 1998, pp.35-59.

[6] Sadako Ogata, "On the Humanitarian Frontlines: Refugee Problems between Changing Wars and Fragile Peace", lecture at the University of California, Berkeley, 17 March 1999, pp.1-6; and "Humanitarian Challenges of Today", keynote address at the 8th International Congress on Infectious Diseases, Boston, 15 May 1998, pp.1-6.

[7] Bas de Gaay Fortman and Berma Klein Goldewijk, *God and the Goods: Global Economy in a Civilizational Perspective*, Geneva, WCC, 1998.

[8] Will Kymlicka, *Multicultural Citizenship: A Liberal Theory of Minority Rights*, Oxford, Oxford UP, 1995.

[9] Cf. R. Williamson, ed., *The Role of Religion in Conflict Situations*, report of a Middle East Council of Churches consultation, 23-27 April 1990, Uppsala, Life & Peace Institute, 1991.

[10] Cf. Riffat Hassan, "A Muslim's Reflection on a New Global Ethics and Cultural Diversity", in *The Power of Culture: Our Creative Diversity*, Amsterdam, KIT Report, 1996, p.2.

[11] See David Little, "Religious Nationalism and Human Rights", in Gerard F. Powers, Drew Christiansen and Robert T. Hennemeyer, eds, *Peacemaking: Moral and Policy Challenges for a New World*, Washington, US Catholic Conference, 1993, p.92; the appeal from the Bosnian religious leaders (Nov. 1992) is quoted in Gerard F. Powers, "Religion, Conflict and Prospects for Reconciliation in Bosnia, Croatia and Yugoslavia", *Journal of International Affairs*, Vol. 50, No. 1, 1996, pp.221-53.

[12] Jeff Haynes, *Religion in Third World Politics*, Buckingham and Philadelphia, Open University Press, 1993, p.64; *Religion in Global Politics,* London, Longman, 1998.

[13] Cf. Sudhir Kakar, *The Colours of Violence: Cultural Identities, Religion and Conflict*, Chicago, Univ. of Chicago Press, 1996.

[14] Peter F. Beyer, *Religion and Globalization*, London, Sage Publications, 1994, p.4.

[15] Douglas Johnston and Cynthia Sampson, eds, *Religion: The Missing Dimension of Statecraft*, New York, Oxford UP, 1994, p.ix.

[16] *Ibid.*, pp.3-6.

[17] Edward Luttwak, "The Missing Dimension"', in *ibid.*, p.13.

[18] Alex de Waal, *Famine that Kills: Darfur, Sudan 1984-1985*, Oxford, Clarendon Press, 1989.

[19] Joanna Macrae, "Purity or Political Engagement? Issues in Food and Health Security Interventions in Complex Political Emergencies", paper for the Humanitarian Policy Programme, Overseas Development Institute, London, 7 March 1998.

[20] Cf. Johan Galtung, *Conflict Transformation by Peaceful Means (The Transcend Method)*, manual prepared by the Crisis Environments Training Initiative and the Disaster Management Training Programme of the United Nations, New York, United Nations, 1998.

[21] *Ibid.*

[22] *Ibid.*

[23] *Peace to the City Newsletter*, Part II, 1 Sept. 1998, Geneva, WCC.

[24] Douglas Johnston and Cynthia Sampson, *op. cit.*, p.5.

7. Poverty and Displacement

Most current strategies to alleviate or eradicate poverty treat economic, social and cultural displacement, risk, vulnerability and violence as *external* factors. Often these factors are understood in terms of the origins or indicators of poverty, but not as an integral part of the worldview of poor, displaced and vulnerable people. Even "actor-oriented" analyses of poverty very rarely focus on how processes of change are assimilated and integrated – or rejected and repudiated – by poor people in the conditions of everyday life.

In this chapter and the next, we focus on how poverty and vulnerability are perceived and what they mean in everyday life. It will become clear that it is almost impossible to express the complexity of concrete perceptions of poverty and vulnerability in just a few concepts. Many poverty studies highlight some aspects of poverty at the expense of others, so that the links between poverty and vulnerability remain invisible. More interrelated approaches are needed.

In this chapter we will particularly relate the concept of poverty to *displacement* and the new "sense of place" which must be developed by poor people who have to cross boundaries in the course of their life. Displacement is usually understood in the physical sense of forcing a group through discrimination, persecution or violence to leave the place where they live. The changing character of war and peace has created a context in which forced displacement is both an aim and a tactic of warfare – for example, in the former Yugoslavia, the Caucasus and the Great Lakes region of Africa. Moreover, the number of stateless people has grown since the beginning of the 1990s as entire populations are deprived of the civil rights they once enjoyed in their country.[1] Our use of the term will not focus primarily on the geographical displacement of people (the inflow and outflow of refugees and migrants, or the growth in mobility created by ever more insecure labour contracts), but on a complex of inter-related dislocations and disorientations in the socio-economic, cultural-religious and psychological-emotional spheres. Certainly the physical movement of people from one place to another remains important, but we seek to go beyond this and examine the outgoing movement or departure from the *position* one had in life and the corresponding changes in orientation.

Poverty and rights-based approaches

Many of the articles of the International Covenant on Economic, Social and Cultural Rights relate directly to poverty – for example, the right to work, including the right to gain one's living by work which one "freely chooses or accepts" (Art. 6), the right to "just and favourable conditions of work" (Art. 7), the right to "social security, including social insurance" (Art. 9), the right to "an adequate standard of living..., including adequate food, clothing and housing, and the continuous improvement of living conditions" (Art. 11), the right to "the enjoyment of the highest attainable standard of physical and mental health" (Art. 12), and the right to education (Art. 13).[2] A United Nations Development Programme policy document calls poverty "a brutal denial of human rights".[3] For the UNDP, reframing poverty in the vocabulary of human rights is linked to implementing the right to development and promoting a vision of human rights as part of sustainable human development. At the same time, as the UNDP recognizes, poverty and inequality can themselves seriously undermine the advancement of human rights by generating violence and civil strife. From a poverty perspective basic human rights must be protected, whether a state is poor in terms of economic resources or not – though, as Willem van Genugten observes, it takes time and money for poor states to build up political, social, economic and legal structures to ensure these rights.[4]

However, it is not only poverty which is humiliating, but also some efforts at development and humanitarian aid which aim to "eradicate", "alleviate" or "attack" poverty. This is especially reflected in cases of development-induced displacement.[5] Poverty must therefore be understood in terms of its core impact – *violation of human dignity* – and the recognition of basic human needs is thus particularly relevant in response to poverty. However, research on poverty over the last three decades shows a tendency to focus on strategies for eradicating or alleviating poverty which are often *instrumentally* linked to available resources and not to poor people's perception and expression of their own needs.

The UNDP has defined poverty as "the denial of opportunities and choices most basic to human development – to lead a long, healthy, creative life and to enjoy a decent standard of living, freedom, dignity, self-esteem and the respect of others".[6] Poverty is thus multi-dimensional and complex. It means, in this sense, the lack of sustainable livelihood. The UNDP's Human Development Report of 1998 goes on to speak of inequalities in consumption patterns and effects, and underscores the need to broaden human development approaches, which aim at enlarging all human choices, towards extending and improving consumer choices as well. On this view, consumption may contribute to human development if it enlarges people's capabilities and enriches their lives without affecting the well-being of others in either the present or future generations. Globalization, however, redistributes opportunities and benefits in ways that lead to increasing social and economic inequality.

Such approaches basically understand poverty in terms of a lack of material and cultural resources which restricts one's ability to socialize. Poverty is a "trajectory" of progressive decline and reduced options in everyday life.[7] Seen in this way, poverty is not limited to those who are traditionally considered to be "the poor". The lack of material and cultural resources can also be experienced by people who take part in all kinds of social or communal activities and who do not feel marginalized. At the same time there can be forms of social marginalization which reduce the opportunities and possibilities of those who are not traditionally thought of as "poor". In other words, poverty and social marginalization are not simply to be identified.

Perhaps the most common image of poverty is the city slum, seen as an undifferentiated and homogeneous habitat for the poor. In this sense, "the city" conjures up depressing realities: abject poverty, crowded and substandard living quarters, crime, child neglect, dependency. Poverty under-stood in this way is often one element in a long list of social woes, alongside crime, violence, drugs trafficking and use, changing ethnic composition of urban areas, conflict and ten-sions, defects in formal schooling and unresponsive welfare systems. Such a static understanding of poverty expresses itself in terms like "slums", "squatters", "compounds" or "social backwardness".

We would suggest a different focus, in which poverty is not just a characteristic of certain groups, countries or shanty towns. On the contrary, our first hypothesis is that the way poverty is lived and experienced by the poor themselves has no predetermined and fixed patterns. Poverty *constantly changes*, affecting people in very different ways, in many different contexts and at distinct moments in life.

The point to be discussed in this chapter is thus how the poor themselves understand internal processes of change in their own environments and how they cope with threats and risks in everyday life. Furthermore, how do such internal processes of change relate to external change in society as a whole, and how are people able to integrate this in their self-understanding in daily life? In this respect, we will not focus on the type of resources which are lacking or denied, nor will we explore the reasons for the diversity among situations of poverty. Rather, we shall try to capture the complexity of the living experiences of the poor. To understand the complexity of poverty requires a dynamic approach to the interaction of different forces. To come to a deeper understanding of what poverty means in everyday life and to explore the interrela-tionship between internal and external processes of change, we concentrate on the subjective experiences and percep-tions of poverty.

Poverty has different faces. Contrary to common opinion, most of the urban poor are *not* just surviving; rather, they organize their lives reasonably. They are not mere victims of declining socio-economic circumstances, but neither can they be simply identified as "agents of change", offering their own solutions for coping with poverty, which is a frequent perspective of anti-poverty research and strategies. The poor are autonomous subjects like everybody else. From this point of departure, the focus shifts to the lives of the poor – their different occupations, the choices they make, their responses to their situation and their reflections on their own living conditions.

Poverty in an *absolute* sense (hunger and famine, risks in everyday physical existence) can be distinguished from poverty in a *relative* sense (having less to spend for daily subsistence than others around one). A distinction may also be made between poverty in a *material* sense and poverty in a *non-material* sense. This is related to an accumulation of objective and subjective difficulties sometimes described as the *multidimensional deprivation* of poverty: on the one hand, lack of income, no work, a limited social network, high rents, debts, inferior education, poor health; on the other hand, playing an insignificant part in social interactions, no real prospects for change, feelings of discrimination, subordination and exclusion. However, not every form of need or of a living at a social minimum can be called poverty. Here the *sustainable* and *structural* character of the situation plays a major role: the longer people live at a subsistence level, depending on a social minimum, the more difficult life becomes.

The concept of *relative poverty* – in relation to whom or to what do people consider their own situation as impoverished? – is gradually changing in poverty research. According to Peter Townsend, one of the leading contemporary theorists in this area,

> people are relatively deprived if they cannot obtain, at all or sufficiently, the conditions of life – that is, the diets, amenities, standards and services – which allow them to play the roles, participate in the relationships and follow the customary behaviour which is expected of them by virtue of their membership of society. If they lack or are denied resources to obtain access to these conditions of life and so fulfil membership in society, they may be said to be in poverty.[8]

Laura Buffoni believes that Townsend and others implicitly link relative deprivation to the *disproportionality* of the poor in their relation to others; and in this sense their approach is based on *inequality*. She argues that insights into inequality do not necessarily deepen insights into poverty.[9]

Poverty research in Europe has indeed focused on notions like "relative poverty", "social exclusion", and "social security", whereas the key concepts for poverty studies in the US have been "underclass" and "ghettoization", and poverty research from the South has highlighted such concepts as "quiet encroachment" and micro-credits. Despite such differences of approaches, there is growing recognition in international research on urban poverty[10] that a conceptual framework is more relevant if it is not the abstract notion of *poverty* which has the central place, but *the poor* themselves. A "people-centred approach" is less concerned with objective indicators (fixing the "poverty line"), and gives more attention to subjects and their perceptions of what it means to be poor.

Socio-economic and cultural-religious displacement

Against this background we may now elaborate the idea of displacement and its intrinsic connection to vulnerability and risk. As we said earlier in this chapter, we use this term not so much in a physical sense as for the socio-economic and cultural-religious dislocations and disorientations poor people experience.

Nevertheless, physical displacement cannot be overlooked. Violent conflicts often lead to forced displacement, as people are uprooted from their home areas against their will. This may be done to create "security zones", or to prevent armed groups from recruiting supporters, or to punish or terrorize ethnic, linguistic or religious minority groups viewed as hostile. Displaced people are often isolated in camps in conditions which resemble detention. Expelled populations are forced to move to unsafe areas in their own or other countries; and even after the conflict ends, many are prevented from returning and are condemned to a life in exile.[11]

Besides violent conflict, human rights abuses are among the main causes for involuntary external and internal displacement of people. During the 1960s and 1970s, international attention was drawn to the resettlement of externally and internally displaced persons in African and Asian countries, as a consequence of civil wars and national liberation struggles. No one foresaw the enormous increase in mass movements of people since the 1970s. Today's large-scale humanitarian emergencies combine

> internal conflicts with large-scale displacements of people and fragile or failing economic, political, and social institutions..., random and systematic violence against non-combatants, infrastructure collapse, widespread lawlessness and interrupted food production and trade.[12]

Socio-economic dislocation obliges people to carry on everyday life outside the boundaries of the contexts which formerly provided identity. It may result from the inadequate functioning or breakdown of political structures, ethnic tensions, poverty or degradation. Under such circumstances, the enjoyment of economic, social and cultural rights is jeopardized. Socio-economic displacement sometimes involves the loss of land and property, due to conflicts over land rights or poorly planned and executed development projects that render certain areas uninhabitable.[13] According to the UN Committee on Economic, Social and Cultural Rights:

> International agencies should scrupulously avoid involvement in projects which, for example... promote or reinforce discrimination against individuals or groups contrary to the provisions of the Covenant, or involve large-scale evictions or displacement of persons without the provision of all appropriate protection and compensation... Every effort should be made, at each phase of a development project, to ensure that the rights contained in the Covenant are duly taken into account.[14]

Cultural-religious displacement means that everyday life has lost its former points of reference, those powerful orientations indicating what is possible and not possible, what the life-rules are, what is sacred and profane, what has sense and what is nonsense. Experiences in everyday life can no longer be integrated within the self-evident coordinates which gave

94

life its sense and meaning.[15] In everyday life, for most people, all things are changing. They must discover by themselves how to survive in the midst of a diverse and overwhelming range of identities, meanings and life-styles. Everyday rituals and symbols are no longer bound to the fixed orientations which used to form people's identity – the school, the political party, the church – but are in constant change. Anthony Giddens speaks in this connection of *disembedding*, the "lifting out" of people in local contexts from their social relations and institutions.[16]

The term "displacement" immediately suggests the *movement* itself: to have to leave this place, to have to give ground, to re-situate and change from the position one previously had. *Place* evokes people's notions of territory and stability, which are deeply influenced and changed by what happens elsewhere, at other places. The world no longer corresponds to the usual setting in which individuals always moved. Three mutually connected elements can be discovered in the changing meaning of place: the concrete and visible changes at the place itself, the intrusion into local reality of what happens elsewhere, and mediation – the integration of this into concrete experiences and perceptions.[17]

Subjective perceptions of poverty: fractures

What does it mean for people to be socio-economically or culturally-religiously displaced, to "feel different", to have to live their lives in a different way – especially when they cannot see how they themselves can bring change to their situation? What does it imply for people to feel themselves in need compared to others, to feel deficits, shortcomings, failures, to feel discriminated against and excluded because of what others consider as their weaknesses? In one way or another people have to cope with all the tensions they live in. They legitimize their own situation and their behaviour – both to themselves and to others – in different ways, which relate to their own subjective experiences of poverty.

An important approach to subjective experiences of poverty has been developed by Pete Alcock.[18] He observes that poverty takes away from people the means and instruments to work towards their future. Because of what people have gone through in the past – poor health, inadequate schooling, perhaps imprisonment and drug addiction – their chances for a future life that is not marked by illness, lack of education, insufficient pensions and a generally insecure environment are very limited. Such people tend to complain and worry more, to suffer from chronic diseases without getting the medical treatment they need and in general to lack the resources for what is required in their environment. People who already have much to overcome in order to play a role in society are often cheated by the same society, leaving them no hope that society will ever meet their aspirations.

Such people live with *fractures* in their lives which mark their perception of their environment and of everyday reality. When such fractures accumulate, there is at least a temporary risk of poverty.[19] For example, someone who has had severe health problems in the past is much more likely to face the present feeling vulnerable, abused and neglected. Moreover, poverty usually forces the poor to live in neighbourhoods which put them at high risk of rapid physical deterioration or involuntary displacement.

Relevant here is the much-discussed concept of a *culture of poverty*, elaborated by Oscar Lewis in the 1960s, originally in Marxist terms.[20] Lewis demonstrated that poverty is a system, a structure, a culture, as well as an internalized attitude. He saw poverty not only as a complex economic and social reality but also as a cultural reality. While recognizing the personal damage which the poor suffer from injustice and deprivation, he affirms that this does not prevent them from living and orienting their own lives. The poor develop coping strategies which allow them to come to grips with their own circumstances; and Lewis identifies a set of positive creative and adaptive mechanisms which are socially constructed by the poor in their everyday lives.

Subjective experiences and perceptions of poverty are extremely heterogeneous. The sense of being useless and disposable, of failure and error, of constant disorientation, uncertainty and shame because there is no exit, touch off a jumble of bad feelings, which may often be hidden in order to avoid the pain. People in such situations get the idea that others look down on them because they have no work or only temporary work, because they cannot pay their bills or their rent, because their relationships with others so easily fall apart. Some feel they are not part of the rest. The sense of living a futile life, always displaced and disoriented, attacks self-confidence and self-respect, decreases the enjoyment of life, embitters and exasperates people, may even make them feel guilty about their own situation. All of these are serious violations of their human dignity and sense of being human.

Traditional and alternative coping strategies of the poor

Current poverty research often understands the strategies the poor adopt to cope with their situation in terms of *risk reduction* – meeting their needs by cutting down consumption or depleting already too-scarce resources. In everyday life this may translate into working longer hours, selling personal belongings for cash, sharing living space with relatives and friends, buying low-quality food and clothes, reducing daily meals and limiting health and education expenditures. Coping strategies offered by states and the World Bank – such as community development, income generation (micro-credits), "safety nets" to sustain low-income groups and other forms of organized social activity – are also problematic. The common difficulty of such strategies is that the extent of their effectiveness remains unclear. All of these strategies are basically *adaptive*. They are oriented towards lacks and shortages, and rarely create conditions for a fundamental change in the person's situation or position.

The problem with such generalized accounts of coping strategies is that they are imprecise and limited, based on a homogeneous perspective which does not do justice to differences in experiences of poverty, differences in perceptions and worldviews or divergencies in coping with the situation of being poor.

It should be emphasized that most activities undertaken by the poor, as by everyone else, are rooted in *routine*. People cope with current, everyday problems on the basis of more or less successful experiences in the past. The term "coping *strategy*" should be distinguished from such routine-based forms of coping. We use the notion of "coping strategy" to refer to some sort of coherent approach of concrete and purposeful efforts to improve living conditions, though the notion of a well-developed strategic blueprint for day-to-day life should not be overstated.

Coping strategies which are in line with subjective perceptions of poverty often focus on *capabilities and empowerment*, which support the abilities and competencies of people to reduce their vulnerability to change and risk and to create new prospects for the future. Such strategies include developing the capacity to deal with money, to relate and communicate with others, to live with stress and uncertainties in work and society, to deal with bureaucracy.

One critique of such approaches is that notions like "competencies", "social capital", "capacity-building" and "empowerment" seem inevitably to involve *social engineering*, which even with the best intentions interferes from the outside. But there are other difficulties as well. One may ask whether such strategies are sustainable in the long run. How long can people reduce consumption without damage? Moreover, stretching resources is always linked with relating to family or community structures. But such solidarity among different strata of the poor cannot be taken for granted: in heterogeneous and mobile urban communities families tend to compete when resources are scarce, and in homogeneous communities such strategies often create or reinforce paternalistic relations of dependency on problem-solvers from the inner circle of family or neighbourhood. The evidence of solidarity and standing up for each other, certainly in urban areas, has strongly diminished: shanty towns once seen as homogeneous are now heterogeneously composed by the continuous ins and outs of different parts of the population. Last but not least, in such coping strategies the social or communal networks which extend beyond kinship and ethnicity usually remain casual, unstructured and non-political. In other words, such strategies reflect the absence in contemporary society of structures that would sustain them over time: they rarely result in social action or group activity.

Coping strategies for economic, social and cultural rights

Two instructive examples of community-based coping strategies which highlight economic, social and cultural rights come from the Peace to the City campaign, part of the World Council of Churches' Programme to Overcome Violence. This programme was inaugurated in 1994, following an appeal from South Africa, where elation over the successful end to the long struggle against apartheid – supported by churches around the world through the WCC – was tempered by a sobering recognition of the pervasive and chronic violence threatening the birth of a new society. The basic hypotheses underlying the programme were: (1) violent conflicts and wars are best resolved by those living within the situation – peace agreements and conflict resolution cannot survive without support from local communities themselves; (2) the focus should not be on the violence itself, but on making visible the modes of reconciliation and community-building, in order to stimulate sharing and networking, and to give others hope and practical tools to attempt something similar; (3) churches must refuse religious legitimation to policies supporting the use of violence and must strengthen the will and courage of people to resist a culture of violence. Within this framework, the Peace to the City campaign, launched in 1997, sought to respond to the rise of violence by focusing on the city as a microcosm of both the most destructive forms of violence and the most creative initiatives to overcome it.[21]

The first example is Rio das Flores, a housing project launched by Viva Rio, a community group in Rio de Janeiro – one of the seven cities chosen as focal points for the Peace to the City campaign. The United Nations has also cited Rio das Flores in an analysis of habitational projects around the world.

The Rio das Flores community rose from the dust and debris left by the heavy floods which devastated the city of Rio de Janeiro in 1996. The city-wide campaign launched at the time by Viva Rio to provide emergency relief to the thousands of flood victims later developed into a wide-scale community housing project for nearly 300 families who had lost all their belongings during the heavy rains. Working in teams, the flood victims helped to rebuild all the homes in their neighbourhood, and took part in planning councils determining how they wanted to design their new community.

The Rio das Flores housing project was conceived as well to include within its scope the urban context as a whole. An integral part of the project therefore included the setting up of basic community services such as sanitation, health care and educational assistance. The community is also benefiting from other projects coordinated by Viva Rio: the Citizen's Counter, which provides free judicial assistance and conflict mediation, and the Viva Cred investment office, which provides low-interest loans to help start up small businesses.

The Rio das Flores community also participates in the Out-of-School Literacy Programme, which provides students from all ages who were not able to finish their basic education with the opportunity to finish their schooling. Today, Rio das Flores is not only a "success story" for the flood victims who have literally rebuilt their own lives from scratch, but also a small-scale model of solidarity and organization.[22]

Another example, also related to housing, comes from Kingston, Jamaica:

In an inner-city environment, a word spoken out of season – or what is commonly called "informing" – could cause one injury or even one's life. This reality was brought sharply into focus when a woman was alleged to have spoken to the police about where weapons were hidden. Word soon got around that she was the possible culprit; and in reprisal the person at whom she had pointed the finger shot and injured her. This man was subsequently arrested for this crime and put behind bars.

A week after the arrest, the community woke up to the news that overnight juveniles who fancied themselves supporters of the jailed gang leader had set fire to the house in which the woman lived. Unfortunately, the social conditions of the Bennetland area ensure that houses are jammed so closely together that one dwelling cannot burn without those in close proximity being affected. So it was on that fateful night: not only was the woman's house quickly burned to the ground with all its contents, but ten other families were made instantly homeless as the flames quickly engulfed the entire area.

When the embers cooled, approximately eleven families, with an average of four to each household, were standing on the sidewalk in the clothes on their backs – all the material goods they had managed to salvage with their lives.

In response to this series of events, the Community Development Council (CDC) immediately called an emergency meeting which considered the plight of the destitute and strategies for rehabilitation. It was agreed that help should be sought from the member of parliament for the area, as well as the relevant national organizations. The MP visited the area, spoke with the residents and promised to help the displaced families to relocate to an area to be identified within the community as quickly as possible.

In the meantime, the victims of the fire have been staying intermittently with family and friends. The CDC delegation, along with representatives of three of the affected families, also visited the offices of the Ministry of Social Security and Justice to appeal for help. The direct involvement of the MP created an easier channel for the delegation to access the help which was immediately forthcoming. The Ministry of Social Security's instant response was commendation for the organized efforts to secure support for the injured parties and to contribute materials to all the affected.

One week following this incident, the gang leader who had shot the woman in the first place was released from jail. He expressed shock, disbelief and anger at the juveniles' impetuousness which had prompted the action of mass destruction. His code of conduct would have been to direct his action of reprisal towards the woman and her alone; there is honour even among the dishonourable.[23]

An alternative strategy: quiet encroachment

A strategy which is rather different from everyday resistance strategies is followed among some poor people in Cairo, who have introduced a challenge that has been described as "quiet encroachment" – a silent but pervasive advancement on the powerful and the "haves" and an expansion of their own space. Quiet encroachment is cumulative, and it is posing simultaneous challenges to "law and order", the public space and existing property. The poor illegally tap electricity and water, not from their neighbours but from the municipality, in order to force state authorities to extend these public utilities to their neighbourhoods. Street vendors, as part of the informal or parallel economy, set up bazaars which encroach on the business of local shopkeepers while escaping taxes and regulations. Others protect cars parked in the streets, which they control and organize into parking lots through internal networks. Still others quietly claim public lands such as cemeteries.

Such quiet encroachment is not so much a mechanism to ensure survival as a means to safeguard small gains already achieved. This is an open-ended struggle, a way for people to live their lives, without clear leadership, ideology or structured organization. Such strategies are atomic and flexible, but of course constantly risk being overpowered by legal and bureaucratic authorities which they circumvent and resist.[24]

This approach has some antecedents. Michel de Certeau, a pioneer in studies of multi-culturality, social diversity and identity politics, has described everyday life as a place for and source of endless tactics of resistance by individuals and collectivities. The everyday tactics of the vulnerable in society always appear stronger than the strategies of the strongest. De Certeau speaks about the *narrative moment* in everyday life: each story about what happens in everyday life is a journey through both space and time, a road, which can begin in the present and which memory will follow – but which must be mapped by symbols and experiences to be shared. The life-world of the urban poor is located in the tension between two poles: "polemological space", which stands for everyday life, where the poor always seem to lose, where truth is not spoken, where the power of others rules; and "utopian space", where the *possible* is affirmed and re-affirmed on the basis of stories which are told and the disharmonies between facts and meaning are exposed. Some of these stories are religious.[25]

Religion and poverty

The resurgence of religion in the face of secularization is commonly explained – as Michel de Certeau does – in terms of the help religion offers in coping with the hardships of increasing poverty. But is religious revitalization indeed a response to social crises and increasing poverty? Is there a direct relationship between the resurgence of religion and the deterioration of living conditions, the increase of political violence and economic chaos? Although many studies have linked the growth of both Pentecostalism and Islamic fundamentalism to declining social conditions and failed modernization, the paradoxical character of religion resists easy simplifications or generalizations. More careful approaches by religious anthropologists and sociologists have indicated that there is no simple, straightforward connection between economic decline and the upsurge of religio-politics among the poor, although economic conditions certainly play a substantial role.[26]

Pentecostalism, for example, indeed attracts poor women in Chile and elsewhere in Latin America by helping them to face economic difficulties and health problems. It appeals to people who are facing personal and economic crises by helping them to modify former behaviour and practices and to create networks that provide stability when they are in difficult situations. At the same time, it is noteworthy that it is in Costa Rica, the region's most stable country, that Pentecostalism and other forms of Protestantism are growing fastest.[27] Similarly, it is often said that Islamic fundamentalist growth since the early 1990s carries discontent with modernization and post-modernism into a religious tradition. These discontents can be seen in terms of economic failure, political authoritarianism and the inadequacy of the state in meeting basic needs, improving the well-being of society and offering prospects for the future. However, it seems inadequate to explain such religio-political involvement solely in terms of an absence of political alternatives or as a direct consequence of economic disappointment.[28]

Conclusion

Against the background of traditional "adaptive" strategies and alternative "encroaching" strategies, we would stress the significance of several elements for the future international poverty agenda, linking this to an approach focusing on economic, social and cultural rights. The first is, indeed, the challenge further to explore rights-based approaches to poverty, especially from the point of view of economic, social and cultural rights. Second is the need to interrelate poverty and displacement, while distinguishing more clearly those manifestations of poverty which are culture-specific from those which are of a more general nature. Third, more attention should be given to the role of non-poor populations in both sustaining and creating poverty and in eradicating it. Fourth, creative ways should be found to link findings from practice and from research, and to discuss the results of these analyses not only with policy-makers, but also with the poor people concerned.

NOTES

[1] Cf. Sadako Ogata, "Human Displacement in the Decades to Come: Meeting the Needs of Refugees", address to the Ramon Magsaysay Award Forum, Manila, 7 Jan. 1998.
[2] Cf. Willem van Genugten, "The Use of Human Rights Instruments in the Struggle against (Extreme) Poverty", paper presented at the CROP/IISL workshop on Law, Power and Poverty, Oñati, Spain, 11-13 May 1995, p.3.
[3] *Integrating Human Rights with Sustainable Human Development* (1998), p.2.
[4] W. van Genugten, *loc. cit.*, p.2.
[5] Ranjit Dwivedi, "Displacement, Risks and Resistance: Local Perceptions and Actions in the Sardar Sarovar", *Development and Change*, Vol. 30, No. 1, 1999, pp.43-78.
[6] *Overcoming Human Poverty*, New York, UNDP, 1998.
[7] Laura Buffoni, "Rethinking Poverty in Globalized Conditions", in John Eade, ed., *Living the Global City: Globalization as Local Process*, London and New York, Routledge, 1997, p.110.

104

8 Peter Townsend, *The International Analysis of Poverty*, Hemel Hempstead, Harvester Wheatsheaf, 1993, p.36.

9 *Loc. cit.*, pp.112-13.

10 For example, the Comparative Research Programme on Poverty (CROP), in which UNESCO cooperates with the International Social Science Council, which offers space for non-Western researchers with a fragile infrastructure and with less established paradigms, theories and methods in poverty research to develop strategies for poverty eradication.

11 For further elaboration of this, see *Minimum Humanitarian Standards*, analytical report of the Secretary-General submitted to the UN Commission on Human Rights, E/CN.4/1998/87, 5 Jan. 1998.

12 Thomas Weiss and Cindy Collins, "Evolution of the Humanitarian Idea", in *Humanitarian Challenges and Intervention*, Boulder CO, Westview Press, 1996, p.4.

13 Cf. *Questions of Human Rights, Mass Exoduses and Displaced Persons: Legal Aspects Relating to the Protection against Arbitrary Displacement*, report of the representative of the Secretary-General, Mr Francis Deng, to the UN Commission on Human Rights, E/CN.4/1998/53/Add.1, 11 Feb. 1998, paras D.1, E.1.

14 *General Comment*, No. 2 (1990) on International Technical Assistance Measures (Art. 22 of the Covenant), HRI/GEN/1/Rev.1, paras 6,8d.

15 Cf. Anthony Giddens, *The Consequences of Modernity*, Cambridge, Polity Press, 1990, p.140. Giddens affirms that modernity "displaces" – that locally situated life-worlds become affected by global, distant events and processes.

16 Cf. Anthony Giddens, *Modernity and Self-Identity: Self and Society in the Late Modern Age*, Stanford CA, Stanford UP, 1991, pp.187-201, 207.

17 Cf. Mike Featherstone, *Consumer Culture and Postmodernism*, London, Thousand Oaks, New Delhi, Sage Publications, 1991, p.95.

18 Pete Alcock, *Understanding Poverty*, London, Macmillan, 1993.

19 Godfried Engbersen and Erik Snel, "Armoede in Perspectief", in G. Engbersen, J.C. Vrooman and E. Snel, eds, *De Kwetsbaren: Tweede Jaarrapport Armoede en Sociale Uitsluiting*, Amsterdam, Amsterdam UP, 1997, p.23.

20 Cf. David L. Harvey and Michael Reed, "The Culture of Poverty: An Ideological Analysis", *Sociological Perspectives*, Vol. 39, No. 4, 1996, pp.465-96.

21 On the Programme to Overcome Violence, see Margot Kaessmann, *Overcoming Violence: The Challenge to the Churches in All Places*, Geneva, WCC, 1998; on the Peace to the City programme, see Dafne Plou, *Peace in Troubled Cities: Creative Models of Building Community amidst Violence*, Geneva, WCC, 1998. The seven cities taking part in the Peace to the City campaign are Belfast (Northern Ireland), Boston (USA), Colombo (Sri Lanka), Durban (South Africa), Kingston (Jamaica), Rio de Janeiro (Brazil) and Suva (Fiji).

[22] "Bulletin from Rio de Janeiro", POV-1, 18 Sept. 1998, Geneva, WCC.

[23] "Bulletin from Kingston, Jamaica", *ibid.*, Aug. 1998.

[24] Asef Bayat, "Cairo's Poor: Dilemmas of Survival and Solidarity", Middle East Report, MERIP (Middle East Research and Information Project), 1997.

[25] Michel de Certeau, *The Practice of Everyday Life*, Berkeley CA, Univ. of California Press, 1984, pp.9,41.

[26] Cf. Ahmed Akbar and Donnan Hastings, eds, *Islam, Globalization and Postmodernity*, London and New York, Routledge, 1994; Laura Guazzone, ed., *The Islamist Dilemma: The Political Role of Islamist Movements in the Contemporary Arab World*, Berkshire, Ithaca Press, 1995.

[27] See Barbara Boudewijnse, Andre Droogers and Frans Kamsteeg, eds, *Algo mas que Opio: Una Lectura Antropológica del Pentecostalismo Latinoamericano y Caribeño*, San José, Costa Rica, Departamento Ecumenico de Investigaciones, 1991.

[28] Cf. Jeff Haynes, *Religion in Third World Politics*, Buckingham and Philadelphia, Open University Press, 1993, pp.35-36,42; and Malcolm Waters, *Globalization*, London and New York, Routledge, 1995, p.130.

8. Vulnerability and Risk

More and more of the world is being sucked into a desolate moral vacuum. This is a space devoid of the most basic human values; a space in which children are slaughtered, raped and maimed; a space in which children are exploited as soldiers; a space in which children are starved and exposed to extreme brutality. Such unregulated terror and violence speak of deliberate victimization. There are few further depths to which humanity can sink.[1]

Graça Machel

Situations of internal violence and conflict create particular vulnerability for certain groups: the poor and displaced; women, who may be subject to sexual violence and exploitation; the aged, who depend on the care of others; and especially children. In Africa, for example, infant and child mortality are at least ten times higher among displaced populations than elsewhere on the continent, accounting for one-fifth of its total child deaths.[2]

Poverty and vulnerability, though linked, are not identical. Those who are the poorest are not necessarily also the most vulnerable; and not all vulnerable people are necessarily poor. Poverty basically points to living with lacks, shortages or needs, while vulnerability can be seen as living with risks, not being able to cope with these risks, and thus facing a life of uncertainty and stress. In this sense, the notion of vulnerability is broader than poverty. The two realities also have different consequences in everyday life and elicit different forms of coping.

This chapter seeks in the first place to explore the concept of increasing *socio-economic vulnerability*. While the term "vulnerability" is used in environmental studies, HIV/AIDS surveys and publications on humanitarian intervention and humanitarian assistance, rarely is the focus on the particular socio-economic dimensions and implications of vulnerability. Second, this chapter aims to contribute to an understanding of *poverty in relation to vulnerability*. Disaster and hazard studies sometimes make a link between poverty and vulnerability,[3] but this is seldom done in international poverty research. The relations between poverty and vulnerability are complex, and more attention in poverty analyses should be devoted to understanding risks in people's lives and their possibilities and impossibilities for coping with unforeseen circumstances.

Everyday life, social vulnerability and risk

The interweaving of vulnerability and poverty is an indication of the multi-dimensional nature of poverty. To speak of vulnerability emphasizes the subjective, relational dimension of people's everyday lives with tensions and risks. The concept thus has a strong emotional element rather than purely cognitive contents. For example, if poverty is related to social exclusion, vulnerability is more closely linked to the *sense of being excluded.*

How do people perceive and express socio-economic vulnerability? First of all, vulnerability points to being susceptible to harmful circumstances: being injured, feeling damaged, wounded, hurt, fearing mutilation. The injury need not be an experience of the present; vulnerability can also arise from living now with the scars of harm suffered in the past. There are circumstances in the past which continue to hurt, which have ruined one's self-image, which have damaged or broken one's expectations and perspectives in everyday life. Such circumstances are not only *external* – for instance, the experience of institutional or structural violence – but may also have *internal* characteristics, related to how people deal with themselves or others around them. Vulnerability can express itself in silencing or hiding oneself, in experiencing the surrounding world as hostile and threatening. For some, the feeling of mutilation and disfigurement, of violation of self-respect and personal identity, can be so deep and painful that they even try to make their own lives overlooked by or invisible to others.

Vulnerability, we have said, means living with risks. The term "risk" points to the possibility of things going wrong, and is thus related to the threat people feel that they can no longer cope with their situation. In everyday life, risk is the probability that some kind of harm or loss will occur – a disaster, poverty, being abused. Living with risks in everyday life means being unable to handle sudden and unforeseen deteriorating situations, feeling unprotected and insecure, seeing no real ground for thinking that one can cope with future risks. In this sense, risk stands for the danger of losing access to food, income, health care or other elements in life which one values. Intensifying the experience and perception of risk in vulnerable lives is the fact that risks can interact, generating a spiral in which one problem leads to another. In summary, we may identify at least three different components to a situation of risk: (1) a clear *identification* of what can be lost (health, property, a job, quality of life); (2) the *probability* of suffering damage or loss in the present; and (3) the *anticipation* of further evil in the future.

Risk always takes place in a social context. It increases or decreases depending on the support that is available. Thus, the way in which family, friends, social networks, institutions or government agencies deal with vulnerable people can augment or diminish the risks they face. Moreover, the ways in which people themselves cope with risks in their everyday life vary according to both the nature of those risks and the contexts in which they live. A distinction may be made between living with *basic or structural risks*, when people experience vulnerability over a long period of time, and *changing risks*, to which people feel particularly vulnerable under certain circumstances.[4]

Many discussions of risk seek to identify those people who are most likely to experience vulnerability and focus on "risk factors" or "risk indicators". Often these factors are presented as a kind of checklist, which may be used to single out certain people or groups for external intervention – without those at risk being given a say in the proposals for risk reduction. In our opinion, it is more important to enquire into *why* certain events or processes constitute risk factors.

Vulnerability and worldviews: meaning and relevance

The ways in which people perceive risk and experience uncertainty and stress are related to their *worldviews*. Uncertainty and stress not only influence how people characterize the risks in their lives, but also play a role in their concerns about the probability of risk. Their worldview may offer guidance and orientation to balance and manoeuvre in the complex and threatening situations of everyday life.

The connection between living with vulnerability and people's perception of their own vulnerability offers a broader perspective on risk, uncertainty and stress. In our view, vulnerability cannot be disconnected from people's internalization of the circumstances in which they are living and the changes they are going through. As long as there is no uncertainty or threat, people's worldview may go largely unnoticed and taken for granted. But when circumstances change – abruptly or over time – people's worldview and existing points of orientation can be affected by doubt and fear.

It is useful to distinguish three dimensions in the concept of vulnerability. First, there is a *descriptive* dimension, which denotes vulnerability as something which is currently happening; second, the *causal* dimension links vulnerability with the situation that precedes it; third, the *normative* dimension orients vulnerability towards the future, to what has to be done. In a descriptive sense, vulnerability may be seen as a destabilizing event or process, one which throws everyday existence out of balance and threatens disruption, damage or destruction. In a causal sense, vulnerability points to a situation of continuing tensions in which a person, group or society is living as a result of the impact of external or internal forces. In a normative sense, something must be done about this tension, because the actors are not able or do not feel able to cope with it.

We may now describe vulnerability more precisely as an event or a process which relates to the risk of physical or socio-psychological mutilation and damage, or which includes the threat of an acute, disastrous and dangerous situation that may generate injury, but which cannot be handled by the actor or actors, thus resulting in the threat of an intense loss with little or no possibility of recovery. This description of a combination of interacting elements approaches vulnerability more as an event or a process than as a circumstance or a situation. Vulnerability is thus a crisis-like occurrence, involving a harmful situation, which is the result of a series of prior events and which – in its turn – affects the future. Above all, vulnerability points to the gap between the capacities of those who are vulnerable and the concrete requirements of the situation.

From this angle, vulnerability is seen to have three different dimensions: (1) the risk to be confronted, with its stresses and shocks; (2) the lack of the capacities and resources needed to cope with such a situation; (3) the threat of serious harm or loss and the impossibility of recovery.[5] The most socially vulnerable people or societies are those exposed to critical or disastrous circumstances, with the most limited capacity of coping, the most severe suffering and the least prospects for recovery.[6] The common answer to this situation in development efforts is to try to reduce people's exposure to such risks, while strengthening their capacities for coping and broadening their prospects for recovery.

In this sense, vulnerability has explicitly time- and space-related dimensions. It can be both *acute* and *chronic*. Acute vulnerability arises sporadically out of an unexpected event or chain of events; the chronic dimension involves an inherent sense of crisis and lack of opportunities and defences. The concept of the sporadic underscores external factors, whereas the chronic dimension reflects the internal sense of crisis. Acute and chronic vulnerability can however coincide.

With this background we can now relate the meaning of social vulnerability more closely to people's *worldviews*. In the first place, people's perceptions are rooted in their own environment, where grave disasters can suddenly happen, or where there is a permanent crisis, which elicits fear of continuous confusion and chaos. In such cases, regardless of whether the danger becomes reality or remains at the level of a constant threat to daily life, the question of *meaning* – and thus worldview – is at stake. People's worldviews, which offer guidance and orientation to move in reality, are strongly influenced by changing circumstances and relationships. When everyday life is susceptible to uncertainty and mischief, it touches the core of the vulnerability of people's worldview as such: Why do harm and injury threaten or happen? How can life proceed?

Vulnerability and the (im)possibility of coping

The question is thus how people cope with their vulnerability. How do they handle encroaching difficulties and tensions in daily life? How do they protect themselves and others? How do they try to reduce some risks – while perhaps consciously increasing other risks? The feeling of not being able to get out of a situation, that life is beyond one's control, can be paralyzing. Living with the idea that a painful reality or threat will continue for the rest of one's life casts a shadow over daily life and throws up a permanent obstacle to company with others. The need to keep going, to fight for self-respect and self-esteem, is much more difficult to fulfill in vulnerable circumstances – so much so that meaning-giving words and gestures embedded in local knowledge from the past may disappear. Put in objective rather than subjective terms, this creates a structural incapacity to give meaning to one's future.

In such vulnerable environments, where life seems worthless and people's identity is at risk, where paralysis prevails, it is often impossible for people to escape from the situation or to find new possibilities and perspectives on their own strength. Thus we believe that these possibilities must be proposed and offered by others. This runs counter to the view of most coping approaches – that people must break out of their own situation by their own will, capacities and human agency. Yet when people are beyond speech, disabled or demoralized by their situation, unable for whatever reason to cope with risks, tensions and uncertainties, then there is no other way but for others to propose words and gestures, attitudes, interpretations, perspectives. Under such circumstances, it is cynical to reorient people towards themselves.

Our point is that in dealing with subjective experiences of vulnerability and the impossibility of coping, a certain *distance* from people's own biography and their concrete life-worlds must be created. Other words, other images, other stories are needed. These could be described (to borrow a term from Hannah Arendt) as *illuminating stories.*[7]

The feeling of being unable to cope with everyday life expresses itself in a language which paralyzes by powerlessness. Therefore, it is destructive to expect people in such situations to find hope all by themselves, to recall life-giving memories by themselves, to cope with breakdowns purely on their own, to find their own means and build their own capacities to handle their situation.

Moreover, when vulnerable people have to give words and meaning to their own experiences of vulnerability all by themselves, there is always the danger of their becoming entirely bound up in themselves, and thus remaining vulnerable in the sense they already feel. Vulnerable people are thus made the prey of the immediacy of their own experiences. When people themselves are not able to cope with vulnerability and cannot find a way to overcome their own situation, the problem cannot be resolved simply by managing the risk factors or by capacity-building and empowerment.

An integrative perspective

The impossibility of coping with vulnerability requires an integrative perspective, including different points of view from different cultures and religions, and different languages. Vulnerability exists where the hope that may arise from the situation itself is insufficient, where courage is of short duration and quickly smashed, where speaking often ends in silence or being silenced.

In one of the urban slums in Rio de Janeiro, Brazil, a story is told about a wise old man who knew well what vulnerability is. One day, a young man came to him who was so wrapped up in his pain and sorrow that he no longer knew how to live his life, how to walk, how to look at the world. The old man said to him: "If you cannot continue, then go back to the street and look how others walk." This answer encapsulates a good deal of local knowledge of everyday life. The old man did not oblige the other to stand upright by himself, nor did he neglect his vulnerability, pain and sadness. The young man does not need to be taken up with himself: orient yourself to others, he is told; look at those who walk – as you walked yesterday – and you will walk tomorrow. Moreover, the street takes away the hopelessness of his situation: taken up by street life again, he may be spared further loss of orientation by the others in his surroundings.

To speak words, to tell stories which the vulnerable themselves may not be able to tell, is crucial. Such words meet vulnerability from the outside; and relief cannot in fact always come from within the vulnerable situation. Of course, words from the outside often – not without reason – lack credibility within the situation itself. And the impotence of silence and paralysis always has its own justifications. But to act from the outside when vulnerable people are calling for this means not letting vulnerability have the last word.

Conclusion

We have seen in this chapter how vulnerability creates a new momentum in the field of economic, social and cultural rights. Vulnerability can be understood as preceding, accompanying or arising as a consequence of poverty. We called for a new, integrated approach to poverty and vulnerability, whose point of departure is the acknowledgment that in some environments, coping with the situation by those living in conditions of extreme vulnerability cannot be expected. In such situations, besides resources and gestures, illuminating stories from the outside might be needed. Their most notable effect is that they create a certain distance from the immediacy of the experience and perception of vulnerability, and correct the self-perception of the people that they are irremediably vulnerable. Such words might overcome the fatalistic tendency to look towards the future only with fear and hopelessness.

114

NOTES

[1] Graça Machel, "Impact of Armed Conflict on Children", report pursuant to UN General Assembly Resolution 48/157, Document A/51/306, 1996, para. 3.

[2] Joanna Macrae, "Purity or Political Engagement? Issues in Food and Health Security Interventions in Complex Political Emergencies", paper for the Humanitarian Policy Programme, Overseas Development Institute, London, 7 March 1998, p.2.

[3] Cf. Piers Blaikie, Terry Cannon, Ian Davis and Ben Wisner, *At Risk: Natural Hazards, People's Vulnerability and Disasters*, London, Routledge, 1994, pp.60-61.

[4] On risk as a concept, see Ulrich Beck, *Risk Society: Towards a New Modernity*, London, Sage Publications, 1992.

[5] Robert Chambers identifies two sides to vulnerability: "an external side of risks, shocks and stress to which an individual or household is subject; and an internal side which is defencelessness, meaning a lack of means to cope without damaging loss"; "Vulnerability, Coping and Policy", *IDS Bulletin*, Vol. 20, No. 2, pp.1-7.

[6] Cf. H.-G. Bohle, T.E. Downing, J.O. Field and F.N. Ibrahim, eds, *Coping with Vulnerability and Criticality: Case Studies on Food Insecure Peoples and Places*, Freiburg Studies in Development Geography, Saarbrücken, Breitenach, 1993, p.9.

[7] Cf. Hannah Arendt, *The Human Condition*, Chicago, University of Chicago Press, 1958.

9. Legitimacy and Legality

> Passing a nobleman's land, a beggar asks him: "Whose is this land?" "It is mine," comes the answer. "And how did you get it?" "Well, I inherited it from my father." "And how did he get it?" "He inherited it from my grandfather." "And he?" "From my great-grandfather." So they go on and on until they come to a great-great-...-great-grandfather who lived in the Middle Ages. Here the nobleman replies: "He fought for it!" "Ah!", says the beggar, "shall we fight for it again?"
>
> Old Dutch story

We have earlier mentioned "enabling environments" approaches to human rights. The reality of the world today is that millions of people live in what might be called "disabling environments": misallocation of resources, extreme social and economic inequality and exclusion, violence in and among communities, corruption, anarchy, cultures of domination and submissiveness. In such conditions of abject poverty, extreme vulnerability, famine and other gross and systematic violations of basic human dignity, human rights tends to be a strange and alien element. Conventional human rights strategies, primarily based on juridical mechanisms and the use of legal resources, are bound to fail.

One "disabling" factor is certainly a malfunctioning economy. This has two aspects: economic *ineffectiveness*, in the sense of misallocation of resources, and economic *injustice*, meaning the exclusion of people from access to resources and entitlements to basic goods and services. Our review in chapter 3 of conventional development-oriented approaches to poverty and destitution showed that responses focusing only on market freedom tend to be insufficient if not counterproductive. What is needed is a proper analysis of existing *entitlement systems* – the regularized arrangements in which people's participation in the economy is rooted – and how they function. If the limitation of resources is to be tackled by increasing productivity, this will have to be supplemented by entitlement-oriented approaches.

An analysis of entitlement systems must give primary attention to the role of the state. A practically non-existent or failed state – such as one finds in Somalia, for example – is certainly an adverse environment for the realization of economic, social and cultural rights. On the other hand, the great famine in North Korea during the late 1990s may be seen as a violation of rights by a totalitarian and terrorist state, which uses law and state power to oppress its own citizens. The centralized command state, encompassing the entire economy (and most other spheres of life) and blocking private initiative, has virtually collapsed, having manifested in the former Soviet Union and its allies a total inability to run the economy effectively.[1]

The role of the state is generally linked with the quality of politics and the nature of the government. Crucial here is the question of the control of political power or office. While no political environment is entirely free of corruption, a climate in which corrupt decision-making is permanently taken for granted in everyday life must be judged as totally harmful to the implementation of socio-economic rights.

Another major factor is civil society. In typically adverse environments this is non-existent, since all associations are subservient to the regime. Totalitarian government will naturally provoke resistance. But such resistance is bound to remain rather weak in environments where fatalism or determinism undergirds a culture of resilience and passivity in the face of domination: people accept things as they are. Personal attitudes to power and its use are rooted in culture; thus in analyzing environments regarding the implementation of human rights, cultural factors must be given special attention.

Human rights in adverse environments

Laguna de Bay is a lake not far from Manila, the capital of the Philippines. On its shore is a fishing village. The catch is primarily for local consumption. However, only about a third of the lake is accessible to the locals; the rest is owned by rich individuals from Manila. These "waterlords" have affixed nets to the bottom of the lake, in effect trapping "their" fish in private "ponds". But every once in a while a typhoon sweeps the water across the lake; and the fish escape from the private ponds. "Today God is with us," the locals say. But what about tomorrow? Should the lives of these poor villagers remain forever limited by unequal access to basic resources? Should things always stay as they are? Or might God be assisted a little?

In this context the word "God" is used almost as a synonym with *justice*. Some languages express that conviction in their vocabulary. In Chinyanja, for example, the word for "God" is *Mulungu*, while justice is called *Chi-lung-amo*. God is the upright one and justice means doing God's will.

Today the fishermen of Laguna de Bay have organized themselves in a cooperative which also fights for their fishing rights. In this way they are assisting God in righting the wrong. Their struggle for greater access to the lake is a fight against *legality*, as embodied in the status quo, in favour of *legitimacy*, a generally held conviction requiring what is right and wrong. Here human rights plays a crucial part. These villagers have become aware that they have rights which follow from universal socio-economic rights. Human rights may, in other words, transform a clash of interests as protected by different power positions into a struggle for social justice. Hence, in adverse environments the primary meaning of human rights is to make people aware of what is basically wrong. Cultures of passivity, determinism and submission may thus give way to new forms of initiative and resistance.

What is at stake here are not ordinary subjective claims in the sense of interests protected by law. Behind human rights are freedoms and needs so fundamental that their denial puts human dignity itself at risk. What may seem from the outside to be a simple conflict of distinct interests protected by different power positions is now placed in a normative context, confronting both interests and the use of power with values attached to human dignity. Where positive law is not protecting respect for such freedoms and needs, human rights maintain their character as principles of legitimacy. In other words, where needs meet rights actors become *duty-holders*; indeed, there are no rights without corresponding duties of others. As James Gustave Speth has put it, "the human rights approach to poverty eradication is motivated by duty".[2]

From the angle of legitimacy, the poor are to be viewed not just as people in need but as human beings with dignity and rights.[3] While this may sound self-evident, such a perspective is far from generally accepted. Its implication is that when people get into situations in which their needs are denied in such a way as to affect fundamentally their human dignity, these needs constitute the basis of claims grounded in human rights. A recognition of this link may be found in religion. In Christianity, for example, the claims of the poor are grounded in their rights, while Islam would place the emphasis on the duties of the rich.

Naturally, to be covered by human rights, needs should be of an essential or basic nature, and the reason they are not being satisfied should lie in the lack of possibilities to participate in socio-economic processes connected with the production, distribution and consumption of essential goods and services. Exclusion from such processes, resulting in a denial of basic needs, may mobilize people to an aroused awareness of their socio-economic rights. The key word here is *legitimacy*.

Legitimacy, which has both objective and subjective aspects, relates to *principles*, *means* and *outcome* of the use of power.[4] Legitimacy transforms power into authority. It is based on people's conviction that the way power is exercised over them and the way they are being ruled are *right*, and hence that they are morally bound to obey. It is a combination of human needs with public opinion, political conviction and cultural expression that demands satisfaction of these needs as a condition of *legitimate* use of economic power.

In this light legitimacy becomes not so much a fact as a process. Central in this process is the "public interest" or "common good", in the sense of all that keeps the public-political community together. The public interest is not to be seen as the highest common factor of all private interests: while many thieves might concede that punishment of theft is in the public interest, very few would consider that their own punishment would be in their own private interest.[5] The idea of the public interest is rooted in the idea of society as a living community. Dworkin (who uses the term "integrity") specifies what this means:

- *fairness*, "the right structure for the political system, the structure that distributes influence over political decisions in the right way";
- *due process*, "the right procedures for enforcing the rules and regulations the system has produced";
- *justice*, the right outcome of the socio-economic and political order: "the right distribution of goods, opportunities and other resources".[6]

Using *outcome* as an example, famine, implying gross and systematic violation of the right to food, may be seen as a barometer of legitimacy in the sense of an obvious indication that the use of political and economic power has not been in line with certain basic principles.[7] While famines are correlated with factors that may be explained through entitlement analysis, as Amartya Sen has stressed, their consequences may set in motion entitlement *struggles* against illegitimate use of power.

When disputes arise from clashes of conflicting interests, juridical principles put the confrontation in a normative setting. Such norms were already codified in Roman law. In the sphere of socio-economic rights, there was the rule *nemo de domo sua extrahi debet* (no one may be evicted from his own house). Acceptance by the Dutch supreme court of the occupation by squatters of houses or office buildings which have been left empty by their owners for purposes of speculation goes a great deal further than this by incorporating a right to housing into positive law. Thus, economic and social rights may have an impact on the social and economic relations between people as protected by private or criminal law. But in order for this to happen, those whose claims find their basis in these rights must obviously take action. Through action first, and acquiescence to the new situation later, an illegality may be turned into legality. The roots of this lie in the *legitimacy* of the action, based as it is on resistance against injustice rooted in the wrong institutions and the wrong procedures and manifested in the wrong outcome. K.L. Karst and K.S. Rosenn, discussing Bolivian land reform in 1952-53 under the title "Land Reform First, Then Law", note that "effective land reform in Bolivia occurred when the *campesinos* occupied the great estates, ejecting both owners and administrative foremen".[8] This action was followed by a great deal of legal activity, because the peasants wanted to regularize their new situation by acquiring proper titles.

Distortions in the distribution and control of power, wrong procedures, corruption, inequities in the outcome of processes of production, distribution and consumption of goods and services – all of these factors may pose serious obstacles to people seeking to satisfy their basic, priority needs. While awareness of the economic right to food or to shelter is usually dormant for most people, in adverse conditions these needs activate those rights in the sense of a *legitimate* basis for claims. Such claims will manifest themselves as challenges to the existing economic, political and legal order and may in turn initiate processes to change institutions, procedures and outcomes so that economic, social and cultural rights can be implemented. Through the ages such processes have been set in motion by those who have felt affected by the wrong institutions, the wrong procedures and the wrong outcomes. Think, for example, of the widow in Jesus' parable (Luke 18:1-8), who presses the unjust judge for justice time and again, until he finally gives in. In resistance to what people feel is basically wrong lies the secret of legitimacy as a weapon against legality in situations where needs meet rights.

To put it in slightly different terms, legitimacy is based on the right operation of *entitlement systems*.[9] The implementation of socio-economic rights may thus be perceived as processes of legitimating claims grounded in basic needs – in other words, as distinct ways of protecting needs of people through basic entitlements.[10] In this light, analyzing the entitlement systems behind concrete cases of entitlement failure is a starting point for making economic, social and cultural rights a reality.

Poverty, destitution and entitlement failure

Who gets what – and how? This is a basic question in any socio-economic order. Amartya Sen of India, who received the Nobel Prize in economics in 1998, calls this "the acquirement problem". Acquirement – the term is chosen to avoid the ambiguous connotations of the more familiar word "acquisition" – is the practice of getting access to the necessary resources and the goods and services needed. Sen identifies certain "legal channels of acquirement".[11] Although this notion is essential for the implementation of economic, social and cultural rights, Sen observes that it "is often neglected not only by non-economists, but also by many economists, including some great ones".[12]

Acquirement involves not only people's productive *activities* but also the *titles* on which their access to resources is based and their *rights* to the fruits of production. Thus two people with the same amount of income may be in entirely different positions as far as their claims are concerned. The $100 earned by a farmer who owns his land is worth far more in terms of security within the socio-economic structure than the $100 a seasonal agricultural worker earns in wages. Behind people's participation in or exclusion from socio-economic processes lie different sets of rights and duties which might be characterized as *entitlement positions.*

Entitlement analysis received a strong impetus through Sen's *Poverty and Famines: An Essay on Entitlement and Deprivation* (Oxford, Clarendon Press, 1981), which addresses the problem of entitlement to food. In investigating several cases of famine in Bengal, Ethiopia and the Sahel countries, Sen found no instance in which the explanation was a decline in the availability of food; indeed, during the great famine in the Sahel in the 1980s, the export of groundnuts for the world market continued while people were starving. Each case of famine analyzed by Sen appears to have been caused by *entitlement failure.*

We saw in chapter 2 that Sen distinguishes between production-based and trade-based entitlement. Subsistence economies are typically based on the former: production for one's own needs. While labour productivity is low, socio-economic security may be relatively high. Specialization in production, division of labour and technologies based on economies of scale will increase productivity. But the transition from a production-based to a trade-based economy may negatively affect people's entitlement positions and thus diminish their socio-economic security. Activities to increase productivity imply change, and change produces conflict around rights and obligations. Entitlements analysis offers insight into such processes. Sen bases his entitlements analysis primarily on direct access to resources. Two factors determine the entitlements of a person living in a society whose economy features private ownership and exchange in the form of trade (exchange with others) and production (exchange with nature): the *endowment* of the person (what he or she owns) and what Sen calls *exchange entitlement mapping* – the specification of the alternative commodity "bundles" the person can command for each endowment bundle.

> For example, a peasant has his land, labour power and a few other resources, which together make up his endowment. Starting from that endowment he can produce a bundle of food that will be his. Or, by selling his labour power, he can get a wage and with that buy commodities, including food. Or he can grow some cash crops and sell them to buy food and other commodities. There are many possibilities...[13]

A key word here is the adjective "own": his *own* land, her *own* labour, his *own* shop, her *own* knowledge. Entitled by such ownership, people may engage in transactions with others. The juridical foundations of such entitlement positions are property and contract.

Our discussion of economic, social and cultural rights requires a broader definition of entitlement. By entitlement we understand the possibility to *participate* legitimately – in the sense of participation based on *rights* – in processes of production, distribution and consumption of goods and services. Entitlement is thus a function of both law and power. Power means opportunity, actual command. Law protects in case of dispute. The assumption here is that law results from processes based on the legitimation of power, which of course is not always the case. When law has thus lost its legitimizing function, as we have seen, legitimacy may challenge legality.

This combination of law and power makes entitlement such a precious affair. Entitlement is far more desirable than the occasional claim; thus people try continuously to improve their entitlement positions. They may appreciate the benefits that come from holding a winning lottery ticket or having a temporary job or receiving emergency food aid, but such episodes bring no *structural* improvement of one's entitlement position. Far preferable is the tenured job, fully protected by modern labour law and providing the employee access to many facilities and allowances. Moreover, persons must adjust to external influences that affect their participation in the economy. Thus, more than a given state of affairs, entitlement is a *process*. There is always an interrelationship between rights and duties within a socio-cultural context.

Introducing this qualification "structural" points to the need to look beyond entitlement *positions* – what people can acquire on the basis of their current rights and duties – to entitlement *systems*, which regularize arrangements for access to resources and acquiring goods and services. People find socio-economic *security* on the basis of their positions in these systems.

The relevance of an entitlement systems approach to implementing socio-economic rights can be further illustrated by two distinctions. The first is between *formal* and *informal* entitlement. The latter prevails in what economists call the informal or "hidden" economy. What have been described as *money-metric approaches*[14] to the measurement of welfare in areas where the informal economy is extensive are likely to miss essential elements in people's entitlement positions. This certainly applies to Africa, but the hidden economy is also of crucial importance in the countries of Central and Eastern Europe. Although the legal rules tend to be much clearer in formal entitlement positions, the study of acquirement may in fact be more problematic than in the informal economy, whose essence is actual rather than just officially regulated access. An analysis of informal entitlement from a juridical angle looks not so much at formal rules and institutions but rather takes a *living law* approach – a focus on *actual* instead of *formal* control of power.

In countries where there is no meaningful labour law, for example, workers may still exert a significant influence on working conditions. An historical case in point comes from 18th-century Barbados, where slave-owners could not sell husband and wife separately. This was not because of any formal prohibition or fear of legal recourse, for slaves were merely objects of ownership, not legal subjects. However, the practice of selling spouses separate from each other became impossible because of social realities by which those who formally had no rights informally achieved legitimation of certain power. Behind this "living law", of course, lay the fear of slave insurrections (in sociological terms, "potential collective action"). The manifestation of individually power-less people as a *collectivity* changed social relations. Where formal and informal systems of entitlement co-exist, people's entitlement positions may become highly complex.

A second important distinction is between *primary* and *subsidiary* entitlement systems. The latter come into play only after acquirement on the basis of rights guaranteeing immediate access fails. Examples include social welfare to support people who have no earnings from labour and food aid in case of famine. Naturally, people tend to prefer primary entitlement – access to resources and rights to goods and services on the basis of integration into the community – to subsidiary entitlement as compensation for being marginalized. For example, when the Green Revolution seriously affected the primary entitlement positions of weaker groups in rural areas of India, subsidiary entitlement in the form of food coupons distributed by the state could not be regarded as a satisfactory compensation.[15] Another illustration is the shift of emphasis in government thinking about poverty in

South Africa from "redistribution of incomes..., closing the gap" to "more jobs".[16] Such shifts reflect growing attention to people's socio-economic *rights*.

Entitlement systems

We have suggested that people's unmet needs should be taken as the primary focus for the implementation of socio-economic rights. To get a clearer picture of what lies behind unmet needs, let us look at the core elements of the entitlement systems in which individual and communal acquirement is rooted. There are three main areas here: entitlement based on *direct access* to resources, *institutional* entitlement and *state-arranged* entitlement. Furthermore, in globalized economies, global and regional arrangements such as the World Trade Organization (WTO), the European Union or the North American Free Trade Area (NAFTA) have a continuous impact on people's entitlement positions.

Direct access

Entitlement guaranteeing direct access to resources is based on private (civil and commercial) as well as public (criminal) law, promulgated and enforced by state institutions. Already Adam Smith stipulated "an exact administration of justice" as the first task of the state in a market economy. This is to provide security in the sense of "the predictive states of mind, the *expectations*, that result from assurances given by the law of property and contracts".[17] The person who owns a piece of land may expect to use the fruits it delivers, because society protects property; the person who sells something may expect payment because society provides a regularized means of enforcing contracts. Consequently, it is the law that directly enables individuals to make legitimate claims. It must be borne in mind that the law upon which economic systems of direct private access to resources are based requires a functioning state.

A private law system is well suited for the implementation of fundamental human freedoms (freedom of conscience and religion, freedom of speech and expression, freedom of assembly and association) – provided it operates within the framework of the rule of law; in other words, that the state itself can be summoned for unlawful action. What is further required is a certain amount of human rights activism on the part of the judiciary. This happened in India, for example, with the incorporation into Positive law of the right of defendants in criminal cases to free legal aid (as a result of judgments by the judiciary based on Article 2 of the International Covenant on Civil and Political Rights). Such "judicial activism" may be encouraged by civil society organizations which are prepared to take cases to court even if they regard a favourable judgment to be unlikely. At least, such action creates awareness in the community that it is *rights* which are at stake. This is possible only where the judiciary is independent, creative and committed to human rights. Even so, human rights will not be transformed into actual entitlement if law does not rule. This restriction tends particularly to operate with regard to economic, social and cultural rights. For example, it proved difficult to enforce the Indian Supreme Court's prohibition of bondage of workers in outlying areas where feudal lords rather than the law were in control.

In market economies – based on freedom of enterprise and consumption and free exchange through systems of markets and prices – entitlement guaranteeing direct access to resources plays a major part. Such an economic order is conducive to continuous change, in which one individual, using his or her rights, may benefit more than another. Thus, some people see their wealth growing while others fall into a state of poverty. Private law is not an appropriate mechanism to correct this; and criminal law, the other legal pillar of a market economy, protects property against unauthorized attempts to correct the distribution of wealth. As Anatole France put it: "The law, in its majestic equality, forbids the rich, as well as the poor, to sleep under bridges, to beg on the streets and to steal bread." That private and criminal law are not suitable for protecting economic and social rights is illustrated by the fact that Sen's entitlement analysis was very much inspired by the great Bengal famine of 1943, when he saw people starving on the pavement in front of well-stocked food shops which were being protected by the police.

Yet, economic and social rights may play a role in relations between individuals, for instance through the application of the old legal principle *Quod est illicitum lege, necessitas facit licitum* (necessity breaks the law). In 19th-century France *le bon juge* Malinvaud accepted *force majeure* whenever it was evident that a person accused of stealing food had been hungry at the time. However, this obviously still falls far short of guaranteeing the right to food.

All in all, in cases of famine and other manifestations of structural non-implementation of economic, social and cultural rights, private law acts as a constraint rather than a resource. The challenge is a socio-political one: how to embark on processes of *socializing* the laws of property and contract. Generally, legitimacy – implying a connection with people's legitimate needs – will constitute the basis of *resistance* to the exercise of power.

Institutional entitlement

Institutions constitute another core element in entitlement positions. Indeed, people's access to productive resources and their acquirement of the goods and services they need often comes through the institutions with which they are affiliated. Such institutions may be seen as semi-autonomous: they have their own rule-making capacities and the means to induce or coerce compliance, but they are also part of a larger social matrix which may encroach on their autonomy.[18] Manifold state regulations, for example, are likely to influence decisions made within the institution.

An obvious specimen of a semi-autonomous social institution that regulates entitlement is the tribe, which allocates its members' access to the land and their entitlement to its fruits – usually under the chief's authority – while expecting them to fulfil various obligations. The (extended) family is another. Often, the standard of living of individuals depends not so much on the income they themselves earn but rather on the total income of the household to which they belong and how the household organizes the use of this income.

In modern society many of the institutions in which entitlement is rooted take the form of *associations* rather than communities. Examples are political parties, trade unions, schools, universities, sports clubs, churches and other religious organizations. Business enterprises also tend to function as entitlement subsystems: a job usually means much more than just a transaction in which labour is hired for a certain price. Within enterprises people are likely to acquire substantial and complex entitlement positions. Socioeconomic security – the feeling of being protected against economic threats and risks – is derived from the individual's position within such institutions.

Analyses made of the entitlement bases of different categories of people – peasants in a given area, workers in a certain industry, people in the informal sector in a particular town – reveal that these are to a large extent a matter of organizations, their relative power and their external and internal arrangements. They have their internal rules as well as norms imposed upon them from outside. For example, Sally Falk-Moore's study of the production of expensive ready-made women's clothing in New York shows

> a densely interconnected social nexus having many interdependent relationships and exchanges, governed by rules, some of them legal rules, and others not... Both the legal and the non-legal rules have similar immediately effective sanctions for violation attached. Business failures can be brought about without the interventions of legal institutions. Clearly, neither effective sanctions nor the capacity to generate binding rules are the monopoly of the state.[19]

Thus, an analysis of institutions as bases of entitlement and commitment (duties) should focus not so much on rules *per se* as on the sources of these rules and of effective inducement, coercion and claiming. This appears largely to be a matter of networks and people's position within them. From this angle, *exclusion* may be regarded as a process of "outplacing" people, in the sense of disconnecting them from effective networks.

State-arranged entitlement

The state is a public-political institution of a very special nature, and entitlements arranged through it warrant separate treatment. In regard to the rights to health and to education, the role of the state is essential, since it largely regulates access to medical care and schools, police protection and other collective goods. State law in these areas tends to be *instrumental* – intended to support and promote policies for collective action. Processes of enlarging the collective socio-economic sector within modern market economies are based on interdependence.[20]

But the state of course does not only give; it also takes away – through various forms of taxation. In other words, it rearranges entitlement. Its policies for doing so are not always easily accepted. People may try to circumvent laws by changing the situation on which their treatment by the state was supposed to be based. In reaction to increased tax-ation, for example, they look for ways to raise the level of their deductible costs. Thus it is not the intended effects of instrumental law that predominate but rather its *side effects*. Similarly, in cases of state subsidies, people may try to get themselves into a category that entitles them to a subsidy which was clearly not intended for the likes of them. Thus, for example, persons with a comfortable income may man-age nevertheless to benefit from state-subsidized housing. Meanwhile, many people in lower-income categories do not succeed in acquiring subsidies intended for their benefit. State-arranged entitlement is action-oriented in the sense that citizens seldom realize their entitlements just like that. Citizens who wish to benefit from a subsidy or welfare allowance have to cross at least five different barriers: (1) finding out that there is such a scheme; (2) learning where to get information about it; (3) overcoming embarrassment about collecting the information; (4) understanding the infor-mation and applying it to their own situation; (5) filling out the forms and going through the rest of the bureaucratic procedure. One Dutch study found that nearly one-third of the respondents believed they had submitted a formal request for social welfare while the civil servants concerned felt they had done no more than supply information about it.[21] More broadly, awareness of one's fundamental freedoms and basic entitlements as guaranteed in international law is an obvious starting point for any rights-based approach to intolerable living conditions.

Besides unintended side-effects and attempts to circumvent them, instrumentalist public policies face the simple reluctance of some individuals to obey the law. Thus, alongside the formal (official) sector of the economy and an informal (circumventing) sector, an evading sector (black market) comes into existence. As a result, processes of entitlement become rather difficult to analyze, let alone direct.

It is misleading to say that the realization of economic and social rights requires the state to take positive action whereas implementation of civil and political rights implies a restraint on state power. On the one hand, promotion of civil and political rights requires positive measures to create a socio-economic and political context conducive to respect for human rights; on the other hand, socio-economic rights may be plainly violated by the state. Agricultural policies oriented to producing foodstuffs for the global market while disregarding and destroying domestic food security may clearly lead to the violation of the human right to food.

Where the state does embark on positive measures to implement economic and social rights, it is better to focus on improving existing entitlement positions rather than to create alternative mechanisms based on state bureaucracies. Here we may recall the general preference for *primary* as opposed to *subsidiary* entitlement. The latter may be easily affected by the socio-political culture as expressed in the spirit of the day. In the realm of entitlement there are in practice no "acquired rights" in the sense of permanent and standing guarantees by the state. In many countries around the world today, "no-nonsense" policies of "deregulation", "privatization" and "structural adjustment" have had direct and serious effects on the entitlement situation of certain categories of people, bringing with them new violations of economic, social and cultural rights.

We have said that the power of the state may be used not only to establish separate *state-arranged* entitlement systems but also to intervene in entitlement positions based on direct and institutional access. To prevent undue intervention in private and corporate entitlement relations through corruption or tyranny, state power has to be depersonalized. The binding of all power, including that of the state, to law – "not might but right" – is a fundamental principle. Other principles of the state subject to the rule of law – the *Rechtstaat* – are democracy, the accountability and substitutability of those executing state power and the independence of the judiciary from the executive.

Administrative law in a *Rechtstaat* takes three different forms: legitimizing the execution of state power, aiming at certain policy effects and guaranteeing the rights of citizens in the execution of public policies. If the third category is lacking, state intervention may result in a deterioration of people's entitlement positions.

Because the state plays so crucial a role in establishing conditions that either enhance or exclude people's participation in processes conducive to acquiring the goods and services they need, it is logical to focus on state responsibilities in mechanisms for the realization of economic, social and cultural rights. Four questions arise in this context:

– Is there a state and is it functioning? Does the legal system protect legitimate access to resources and rights to the fruits of productive activities? In a failed state a modern market economy cannot work. Is the state strong enough to carry out its policy decisions and to collect taxes?
– Is the execution of state power subject to democratic processes of legitimation or is it authoritarian or even totalitarian? Does the state guarantee fundamental freedoms?

- Does the state limit its function in the economy to creating the right conditions for market institutions to function, or is it all-comprehensive? If the state is limited in an economic sense, does it adequately provide collective goods and services subject to due processes of legitimation of public office?
- How are the relations between the state and the institutions on which people's entitlements depend structured and conducted? What is the quality of relations between the state and civil society?

The fact that all these questions are important when considering strategies for implementing economic, social and cultural rights makes it very difficult to generalize about the operation of entitlement systems and the implementation of socio-economic rights in a local context.

International effects on entitlement

It is not only national states that affect people's direct and institutional entitlement positions. National economies are increasingly affected by the international order. No analysis of entitlement positions can neglect these supra-state arrangements. Regional and global supra-state trade arrangements have the character of structured interventions in people's entitlement positions – affecting prices, for example – rather than assuming the nature of entitlement systems in their own right.[22] It is no coincidence that the Zapatista uprising in the Mexican state of Chiapas broke out on 1 January 1994. The leaders of the insurrection deliberately chose this moment to act because it was the day on which the North American Free Trade Area (NAFTA) came into effect, and they recognized that this newly established trade regime would directly affect the entitlement positions of peasants in Chiapas through its impact on prices.

Thus, the entitlement systems approach presented here may have considerable practical significance in analyzing people's socio-economic security. It may indeed serve as a basis to rethink strategies for implementing economic, social and cultural rights. Naturally, the objective is an adequate structuring of people's acquirement in strong entitlement positions.

Identifying needs, implementing rights: the role of NGOs

To those unable to realize the basic entitlements set forth in Articles 22 to 26 of the Universal Declaration of Human Rights, the law manifests itself as a constraint more often than as a resource for concerted action. "Laws grind the poor, and rich men make the law", goes a 17th-century song.[23] As Amartya Sen concluded from his analysis of famine: "The law stands between food availability and food entitlement." It was this which has stimulated his own subsequent work on strategies of entitlement protection.[24] The question is whether, in the words of John Maynard Keynes, people should always die quietly. Keynes believed not: "For starvation, which brings to some lethargy and helpless despair, drives other temperaments to the nervous instability of hysteria and to a mad despair."[25]

Let us go back here to Sen's situation of Bengali people dying of famine in front of well-stocked food shops. There was of course a good reason for those without access to food to lie down there. Begging at this spot might appeal to buyers with the necessary means of food acquirement (cash); and money collected from the haves could immediately be used to satisfy the need for food. Although the shop-owners could not be identified as primary duty-holders in the sense that they ought to have given out for free the commodities which they themselves had to buy, at that well-chosen spot the rights-holders did confront society significantly with its duties. To relate the right to food of those in need to the duties of others generally demands an insight into the specific *circumstances* of that particular famine in its international, national and local contexts. Such an analysis in context was in fact Sen's focus in *Poverty and Famines*.

Entitlement, we repeat, is a matter of both power and rights. Since it is unlikely that power will be fairly distributed from above, it must be acquired through concerted collective action by those who lack the possibilities to get their claims realized. The action taken by the fishermen in Laguna de Bay is indicative of an alternative approach to development: development from below, or development as *emancipation*. Many other examples could be cited: the action of the *sem terra* movement in Brazil in the 1990s – in which thousands of landless people illegally occupy land as squatters and then begin an often successful struggle to get their titles recognized – is one of the best-known cases.

Addressing economic injustice is of course no more than a first step in efforts aiming at redress. Despite the brave words of the beggar in the old story cited at the beginning of this chapter, it is unlikely that he could realize land reform on his own. Implementation of economic, social and cultural rights requires concerted action by all actors involved. In such efforts the natural orientation is towards social rather than legal change. Yet it is important for those involved in entitlement-oriented development through "self-help" action against positive law to base the steps they take in a universally accepted morality. Here human rights may play an important part, especially social and economic rights such as the rights to work, food, health, education, clothing and housing.

Where people are obviously suffering from the violation of such rights, the starting point is to identify clearly unmet needs. In the first place this involves the people themselves – and some have been taught through the ages to deny their own needs. Processes of *conscientization* can help them to find spiritual sources of protest in their own cultural environment while developing their own ways of expressing feelings of contention. Churches and other non-governmental organizations working in this field should be aware that the languages of resistance used by people in need have their roots in local culture and religious spirituality and do not necessarily reflect a human rights discourse. But once legitimate needs have been identified, it may be important to seek a clear human rights profile. This implies *awareness-building*, enhancing people's recognition and understanding of their basic freedoms and entitlements. Human rights *educa-*

tion is thus fundamental to any strategy of human rights *implementation*.

Involvement from outside in efforts to redress injustice begins with an existential feeling of being *affected*, fundamentally moved in the depths of one's being. In such processes of activating human conscience, religious convictions and worldviews play a crucial role.

Mechanisms of turning away

Humanity has of course developed powerful mechanisms to avoid being affected by the needs of others. Perhaps the most common is the reversal of responsibilities: blaming the poor themselves for their own destitution. "You know, these people are poor because they want to be poor!", we once heard a government official say about the inhabitants of the slums of Tondo in Manila. In this way poor people are seen as offenders rather than victims; and since they disturb law and order they are best isolated in the workhouses of former times or the shanty-towns and slums of today.

Another mechanism of turning away from social injustice is to see poverty as an inevitable fact of life, a simple basis for economic calculation. In this way the poor may even become objects of exploitation rather than mere neglect: they are people whom one can hire for less than subsistence wages while setting them to work in intolerable conditions.

A third way of avoiding the fate of the poor is through escape: simply closing one's eyes. Reading the newspaper or watching television, one can concentrate only on the diversions: sporting events, tabloid gossip and the endless stream of advertisements which call on us to see life as just leisure and pleasure.

Finally, our duty in response to the needs of the poor may be averted by "deporting" them, fully delegating responsibilities for them to humanitarian organizations such as Oxfam, the church aid agencies, Médecins sans frontières and the like. The challenge for such agencies is of course to do their work in such a rights-based perspective that people in more privileged positions become aware of their responsibilities rather than averting these. A good example here is the threat by European trade unions and political parties of a consumer boycott of Chiquita bananas when it was feared that the company might lay off thousands of workers who were not needed because the plantations in Central America were flooded – a far different reaction from sending relief aid to people who have lost their jobs.

One of the most successful long-term instances of supporting local resistance to oppression based on human rights instruments was the Human Rights Resources Office for Latin America (HRROLA) established by the World Council of Churches (WCC) following the coup d'Etat of General Pinochet in Chile in 1973. Over the next two decades it based its involvement throughout Latin America and the Caribbean on a combination of four different approaches, which should not be seen as consecutive stages in a process but rather as the four corners of a net that can be tightened only by pulling from all sides together: *analysis, advocacy, assistance* and *action*.

A "four A's" strategy

The first element of an integrated approach to human rights implementation is a thorough *analysis* of the institutions, procedures and outcomes behind economic injustice. In this book we have emphasized the use of entitlement systems analysis. Such studies should attend not only to the distribution of local economic power but also to the international economic order. For many countries today – Mozambique and Egypt, to mention only two – a major constraint on implementing economic, social and cultural rights is their foreign debt servicing. Excessive debt, as we have seen, burdens the ability to provide basic social services, health care and education. The eighth assembly of the World Council of Churches in Harare in 1998 correctly put great emphasis on the issue of debt cancellation.[26]

Where needs meet rights, international power relations must also be confronted by the norm of basic human dignity. In analyzing this international dimension of the implementation of economic, social and cultural rights, attention should also be paid to how national and local institutions interact with multilateral institutions and other lenders. There are international as well as domestic responsibilities for the debt predicament in which many countries currently find themselves. The challenge here is to "forgive" while at the same time making sure that the sinners "go and sin no more".

Analysis provides the basis for any timely identification of needs. In the context of civil strife, a striking recent example of such an approach is the International Crisis Group of Mort Abramovitz. In any situation in which this group notes the need for early warning, it thoroughly analyzes the tendencies towards civil war as well as the possibilities of avoiding such disaster. From such a well-documented and argued base, the group then puts pressure on governments to embark on early action. *The Economist* notes two important trends in this strategy:

> The first is that humanitarians of various kinds are thinking bigger than they used to. Human-rights watchdogs began by documenting torture; now they press governments to impose sanctions on the torturers. Aid organizations began by handing out disaster relief; then they moved into longer-term development, hoping to make future missions unnecessary. In his own way, Mr Abramovitz has made the same pilgrimage, from dealing with disasters to addressing their cause...
>
> The second trend behind Mr Abramovitz is that government and multi-government bureaucracies are ceding power to nongovernmental organizations... He has spent most of his career in government..., but he preferred to set up the International Crisis Group, believing that an outside organization might prove more influential than a senior government official.[27]

Abramovitz's ways of alerting duty-holders can serve as a useful model for churches and other non-governmental organizations active in the field of poverty and destitution. Analysis which alerts is one foundation of strategies at the intersection of needs and rights. Another is *assistance*. Naturally, victims of human rights abuses – whether of a civil-political or of a socio-economic nature – seek compensation, healing, rehabilitation and redress. In the area of socio-economic rights we have already touched on a delicate dilemma in this connection. If, for example, people lack education, the response of providing educational facilities may impede *collective action* to demand the state to organize education for everyone. At a minimum, the *legitimacy* of people's unsatisfied basic needs should continue to be stressed in order to maintain a human rights profile.

Advocacy means speaking out: exposing human rights violations while linking them to clear responsibilities on the part of duty-holders. Naturally this must be connected with lobbying and *action* based on human rights networking. Human rights education may serve to set poverty and destitution clearly in the context of the violation of socio-economic rights. Awareness on the part of both rights- and duty-holders may create the expectations in society which legitimate unmet needs as a basis for claims grounded in rights. Pressure to get these claims honoured should aim at *implementation*. In this difficult process, in which many constraints will have to be overcome, coordination and cooperation between multiple actors is required: the people themselves, non-governmental development organizations in the field, foreign donors and (international) non-governmental organizations engaged in human rights implementation. Where needs meet rights, all "actors" become duty-holders.

NOTES

[1] See Bas de Gaay Fortman, "Is Socialism Possible?", *Sociological Affairs*, Vol.1, No. 1, 1998, pp.97-107.

[2] James Gustave Speth, "Poverty: A Denial of Human Rights", *Journal of International Affairs*, Vol. 52, No. 1, Fall 1998, p.287.

[3] See Bas de Gaay Fortman, "Sitting Back in Horror: Intra-State Collective Violence in a Global Context", Annual Day Address, The Hague, Institute of Social Studies, 1994.

[4] See Bas de Gaay Fortman, "Is Democracy Possible", *Sociological Analysis*, Vol. 1, No. 3, 1998, p.65.

[5] Cf. Bas de Gaay Fortman and Berma Klein Goldewijk, *God and the Goods: Global Economy in a Civilizational Perspective*, Geneva, WCC, 1998.

6 Ronald Dworkin, *Law's Empire*, London, Fontana, 1986, p.404.

7 See Alex de Waal, *Famine Crimes: Politics and the Disaster Relief Industry in Africa*, Oxford, James Currey, 1997.

8 K.L. Karst and K.S. Rosenn, *Law and Development in Latin America*, p.650.

9 See Bas de Gaay Fortman, "Beyond Income Distribution: An Entitlement Systems Approach to the Acquirement Problem", in J. van de Linden et al., *Theory of Income Distribution: Heterodox Approaches*, Cheltenham, Edward Elgar, 1999, pp.29-75.

10 Cf. Bas de Gaay Fortman, "Van Nood naar Recht: Veertig Jaar Recht op Voedsel", *Internationale Spectator*, Vol. 43, No. 3, 1989, pp.157-60.

11 Amartya Sen, *Hunger and Entitlements*, Helsinki, World Institute for Development Economics Research, 1987, p.8.

12 Amartya Sen, *Food, Economics and Entitlements*, Helsinki, World Institute for Development Economics Research, 1986, p.5.

13 Amartya Sen, *Poverty and Famines*, pp.45f.

14 See L. Hanmer, G. Pyatt and H. White, *Understanding Poverty in Africa: What Can We Learn from the World Bank's Poverty Assessments?*, The Hague, Institute of Social Studies, 1996.

15 See V. Ramprasad, *The Hidden Hunger: Food Policy in India and its Impact on Entitlement*, Penang, Third World Network, 1990.

16 R. Mogotlane, "Developing South Africa in Peace: Migration in Perspective", paper for Pugwash Meeting no. 218, Lahti, 1996, p.3.

17 K.L. Karst and K.S. Rosenn, *op. cit.*, p.637.

18 See Sally Falk Moore, *"Law as Process": An Anthropological Approach*, London, Routledge & Kegan Paul, 1983, pp.55-56.

19 *Ibid.*, p.79.

20 See Abram de Swaan, *In Care of the State: Health Care, Education and Welfare in Europe and the USA in the Modern Era*, Cambridge, Polity Press, 1988, p.13.

21 Cited by W. van Oorschot and P. Kolkhuis Tanke, *Niet gebruik van sociale zekerheid: feiten, theorieën, onderzoeksmethoden*, The Hague, Ministry of Social Affairs, No. 16a, March 1989, p.9.

22 Bas de Gaay Fortman and Chris Kortekaas, "Intra-state Collective Violence in a Political Economy Perspective", *Pugwash Annual Proceedings*, London, 1996.

23 Quoted by C. Hill, *Liberty Against the Law: Some 17th Century Controversies*, London, Allen Lane, 1995.

24 Cf. J. Drèze and A. Sen, *Hunger and Public Action*, Oxford, Clarendon Press, 1989.

25 J.M. Keynes, *Economic Consequences of the Peace*, New York, Viking, 1920, p.213.

26 For the assembly statement on international debt see Diane Kessler, ed., *Together on the Way*, report of the WCC eighth assembly, Geneva, WCC, 1999, pp.177-82.

27 *The Economist*, 25 July 1998, p.51.

10. A Few Final Thoughts

This book has focused on people in distress: the poor and displaced, the vulnerable, victims of violent conflict. We have also explored the opportunities for and constraints on implementing economic, social and cultural rights. Where basic needs are unmet or even denied, the daily struggle for livelihood becomes an arena full of tension. Human dignity requires recognition in adequate living standards and access to health services and education. Internationally, these needs have been acknowledged as the basis of primary entitlements of each and every individual. Yet the international human rights agenda has given much more attention to fundamental freedoms – civil and political rights – than to the protection of people's essential needs through economic, social and cultural rights. We have seen that the protection of such needs through law and legal mechanisms suffers from three basic constraints:

- an almost exclusively *vertical* focus on state responsibilities, neglecting the role of other actors as duty-holders (corporations and the international financial institutions, for example);
- a *juridical* method in implementation, principally involving standard-setting, monitoring and enforcement by legal means;
- a focus on *resource constraints* as the primary impediment to a full realization of these rights.

The phrase "achieving progressively" in Article 2.1 of the International Covenant on Economic, Social and Cultural Rights has led to development-oriented approaches towards their realization, in which the people whose lives are characterized by denied human needs drop out of sight. Hence, we followed our critique of market-led and state-led development with a new centre of analysis: *human dignity* and its opposite – *humiliation*. From this angle, two new methodologies had to be introduced. Taking the perspective of people themselves means first of all replacing an external problem-solving attitude (development as a panacea for resource pressure) by a *dilemma approach*. Second, a *needs-led* method initiates the implementation of economic, social and cultural rights in what people themselves experience, feel and express.

Human rights are often discussed as tools that have to be taken up and mastered. If that had been our intention, we might have focused only on the opportunities for and constraints to implementing economic, social and cultural rights. But rather than stopping here, that is where in a real sense this book begins. The focus on human needs brings us to the core of strategies for implementing economic, social and cultural rights: basic human dignity. It cannot be gained or lost, though of course it can be seriously hurt and violated. Purely secular interpretations of dignity are rather limited. It is the world's religions that provide deeper sources for understanding this foundation of human rights.

In intra-state collective violence, religion plays a dual role. On the one hand, it is misused to construct or fortify *us-them divides*. On the other hand, it may be easier to reach people from a religious platform than from an international human rights perspective. Religion can indeed contribute towards conflict resolution. In cases of collective violence, the challenge is to get the real conflict, rather than merely its symptoms, in view. This may provide a basis for strategies of *conflict transformation*. In such efforts people's basic needs are bound to come to the fore, and with that comes the necessity of implementing economic, social and cultural rights.

A focus on human dignity lays the foundation for critical approaches to positive law (existing legality). From the side of the poor themselves, *quiet encroachment* is a strategy which transcends the adaptive coping which continuously reduces one's living standards and depletes resources. In their efforts to secure livelihood, poor people do sometimes succeed in gaining new space.

Vulnerability presents a particular problem. Uncertainty and stress may paralyze people. Narratives from outside may break through this incapacity. Although this is not yet a part of traditional human rights language, it may encourage people to stand upright and regain the self-respect that follows from their basic human dignity.

Although the United Nations Development Programme has embarked upon "enabling environments" approaches to human rights, most of the people in need of implementation of economic, social and cultural rights live in *adverse environments*: productive resources are badly allocated, economic injustice is rife, the state is not subject to the rule of law, violence, civil strife and cultures of domination and submissiveness prevail. In such a context of "non-law" or even "anti-law", human rights cannot easily provide legal support for individual claims to resources and essential goods and services. Yet even here, economic, social and cultural rights may be a forceful weapon to contest power based on access to productive resources. The challenge is to build awareness among the rights-holders and to identify the duty-holders. Where denied needs meet human rights, legality is confronted with principles of *legitimacy*.

In order to understand such processes the notion of *entitlement failure* is crucial. It is through the lack of entitlement positions that human dignity tends to be structurally violated; thus, the systems and subsystems of entitlement need to be properly analyzed in order to provide a basis for human rights strategies that enhance socio-economic rights as *real* human rights, which support legitimate claims to food, clothing, housing, health services and education and have implications at all levels of economic power. In society, politics and the economy, the struggle is directed at those institutions and processes which result in violations of basic human dignity; in a positive sense, the search is for a cultural and institutional environment conducive to a realization of everyone's human dignity.

Transforming the struggle

Implementation of economic, social and cultural rights is a continuous, day-to-day struggle for the poor, the displaced, the vulnerable. The argument presented in this book may well be summarized in terms of transforming this struggle. At first sight, the types of struggle in which the deprived and destitute are caught seem only to be clashes of different interests backed by unequal power positions. But where needs meet rights, such conflicts must be seen in a different light in three distinct ways. Each has direct consequences for how the people involved may experience their realities.

The struggle is deepened

Where needs meet rights, the struggle is *deepened* in the sense of being given a normative setting: the confrontation of power with the rights of people and fundamental principles of legitimacy. For example, people fighting for access to clean water are not just involved in a struggle for economic power that will give them better access to goods and services. The denial of their basic needs for clean water confronts society with its own values. This applies to public policies as well as to business decisions. Earlier, for example, we mentioned the phenomenon of development-induced displacement of people, as in the construction of giant dams for electricity generation. This is the essence of the critique of purely "development"-oriented approaches to human deprivation and destitution. It is not development *per se* but human dignity as the foundation of people's basic entitlements that should serve as a primary basis for public and private decision-making.

Economic, social and cultural rights thus imply *rights-based approaches* to poverty and displacement. Here lies the basis for resistance against the status quo and action based on such resistance. Non-governmental organizations and other actors assisting in these struggles should be aware that people's feelings of self-respect may be expressed in types of discourse different from human rights language. What matters is not the words but the effectiveness of the action elicited.

The struggle is widened

When people's essential needs are being denied, the promotion of human rights broadens the struggle for livelihood to involve the whole local community – agents of government, development and peace organizations, women's and environmental groups, and businesses. Where needs meet rights, "actors" become "duty-holders". This implies that economic, social and cultural rights must be integrated into all activities of such institutions, not just incorporated into specific human rights projects.

Shifting the focus of implementation strategies to extra-governmental activity at the local level, including business, requires approaches which may differ from those used in struggles for civil and political rights. There, the primary focus appears to be on legal resources. Economic, social and cultural rights are oriented to action. Action first, legalization later seems to characterize successful strategies.

States should of course be confronted with their positive obligations to provide basic public services to all and to guar-antee adequate living standards. But economic, social and cultural rights may also serve as a weapon to fight concrete state interventions that result in abuse of people's basic en-titlements. In this connection, the implications of structural adjustment programmes, economic sanctions and the immense problem of external debt demand special attention. The establishment of country committees for economic, social and cultural rights, ombudspersons and regional or sub-regional coordinating committees may be seen as signif-icant steps in this direction. Furthermore, where duty-holders can be clearly identified, concrete violations of economic, social and cultural rights may also be addressed in litigation.

The struggle is uplifted

Finally, where needs meet rights, the struggle for live-lihood is *uplifted*. The adjective "universal" in the term "uni-versal human rights" points to *responsibility*. The situation of those whose unmet needs imply a violation of their basic dig-nity is recognized today as a universal responsibility. The human rights mechanisms established by the United Nations are rooted in the universal human responsibility for the implementation of fundamental freedoms and basic entitle-ments. Yet, no matter how important this international ven-ture for the protection of human rights may be, it will have